THE DEGREE GENERATION

The Making of Unequal Graduate Lives

Nicola Ingram, Ann-Marie Bathmaker,
Jessie Abrahams, Laura Bentley,
Harriet Bradley, Tony Hoare,
Vanda Papafilippou and Richard Waller

With a Foreword by Sam Friedman

BRISTOL
UNIVERSITY
PRESS

First published in Great Britain in 2023 by

Bristol University Press
University of Bristol
1–9 Old Park Hill
Bristol
BS2 8BB
UK
t: +44 (0)117 374 6645
e: bup-info@bristol.ac.uk

Details of international sales and distribution partners are available at
bristoluniversitypress.co.uk

© Bristol University Press 2023

British Library Cataloguing in Publication Data
A catalogue record for this book is available from the British Library

ISBN 978-1-5292-0884-9 hardcover
ISBN 978-1-5292-0885-6 paperback
ISBN 978-1-5292-0887-0 ePub
ISBN 978-1-5292-0886-3 ePdf

The right of Nicola Ingram, Ann-Marie Bathmaker, Jessie Abrahams, Laura Bentley,
Harriet Bradley, Tony Hoare, Vanda Papafilippou and Richard Waller to be identified
as authors of this work has been asserted by them in accordance with the Copyright,
Designs and Patents Act 1988.

Cover design: Nicky Borowiec
Front cover image: AdobeStock/jozefmicic
Bristol University Press use environmentally responsible print partners.
Printed and bound in Great Britain by CPI Group (UK) Ltd,
Croydon, CR0 4YY

FSC
www.fsc.org
MIX
Paper | Supporting
responsible forestry
FSC® C013604

Contents

List of Tables

About the Authors

Nicola Ingram is Professor of Education at University College Cork, Ireland.

Ann-Marie Bathmaker is Professor Emerita of Vocational and Higher Education at the University of Birmingham.

Jessie Abrahams is Lecturer of Education at the University of Bristol.

Laura Bentley is ESRC Postdoctoral Research Fellow at the University of Birmingham.

Harriet Bradley is Emerita Professor at the universities of Bristol and the West of England.

Tony Hoare is a Consultant at the University of Bristol, after retirement from his post as Research Director in Widening Participation.

Vanda Papafilippou is Senior Lecturer of Human Resources Management at the University of the West of England.

Richard Waller is Professor of Education and Social Justice at the University of the West of England.

Foreword

Sam Friedman

The Paired Peers project, from which this excellent book emerges, will surely go down as a landmark study in British sociology. Spanning nearly 12 years, this unique and groundbreaking qualitative research has followed the lives of 90 working-class and middle-class students as they first traversed entry into, and progression through, university and now as they negotiate the precarious and uncertain graduate labour market. Reading *The Degree Generation*, I am struck by the ways in which the latest instalment of this project has once again moved our understanding on. These distinct contributions are made possible not only by the quality and the sensitivity of the analysis undertaken by the team (who themselves come from a variety of different class backgrounds), but also by the unique longitudinal research design undertaken. It is clear, for example, that the research team has built very important and deep relationships with their participants over the years, and this has clearly yielded insights that simply would not have been possible using other methodological tools.

The first of these is the simple observation that labour market futures are not the sole focus of graduates. Sociological and policy work in this area, particularly studies that focus on inequalities of outcome (like my own), tend to overlook the fact that young people emerging from university are not just concerned with constructing a career; rather, they are also building a life. Spending extended periods of time with participants, this simple reality becomes abundantly clear: they are not always making decisions with an instrumental emphasis on career success, occupational status or high earnings; instead, they are thinking about how to forge relationships with friends and family, how to enjoy their leisure time, or how to look after their mental health. This is important because it asks us to reconsider conventional understandings of 'graduate success' and instead think about young people's broader quest to find *meaningful* work and to live a life of, what the authors call, 'personal value'.

Second, however, while this book certainly spotlights a uniquely broad understanding of the graduate experience, it also pulls no punches in simultaneously underlining the corrosive inequalities that stratify the UK graduate labour market. Here, in particular, they highlight how notions of 'graduate value' tend to be tied not only to particular universities and particular degree courses, but also, more broadly, to a certain performance or image of merit. This is rooted, they argue, in the embodied cultural capital (modes of comportment, self-presentation and aesthetic style) inculcated via a privileged class background (and inextricably tied to intersections of race and gender), which are then misrecognized as legitimate by gatekeepers. This, they write in Chapter 9, 'constructs some bodies as a 'natural' fit and others as out of place' in the elite graduate labour market.

Of course, the question that flows from this is: how should organizations, policy makers and government respond to these findings? What can and should be done to address these inequities? It is certainly true that, in recent years, discussions about class have at least begun to take place among many of the UK's key graduate employers. For example, there is now the widespread collection of workforce data on class background. This has allowed employers not only to understand their internal class composition and the class pay gaps or class ceilings that might exist around career progression, but also to see how the class backgrounds of their staff intersect with other characteristics, such as race and gender. Some firms have even taken the step of publishing class background data publicly and setting targets to increase the representation of those from working-class backgrounds at partner or senior management level.

Beyond data, though, there is much more that graduate employers must do to be part of the solution. The most significant of these is to grapple with how 'talent' and 'merit' are defined and rewarded in graduate recruitment. The key point highlighted in this book, as well as other allied studies, is that the identification of merit is often intertwined with the way in which merit is performed (in terms of classed self-presentation and arbitrary behavioural codes) and who the decision makers are whose job it is to recognize and reward these attributes. This is a thorny issue that is hard to tackle, especially where there is contestation within professions about what merit or skill look like. Yet, it is pivotal that employers embrace this contestation, critically interrogate the supposedly 'objective' measures of merit they rely on and aim for a more transparent, inclusive and widely agreed-upon idea of what merit looks like in the workplace.

There are certainly, then, some concrete ways in which graduate employers are tackling class inequality. However, at the same time, it is important to register an important caveat to the celebratory narratives that often surround professional employers' 'social mobility strategies'. This is simply that the interventions they envisage may be a *necessary* part of tackling class inequality in the graduate labour market, but they are certainly not *sufficient*. Fundamentally, this is because they only address one aspect of class inequality, namely, equality of opportunity and the fair allocation of rewards within the workplace. However, as a range of sociologists have argued, including Nicola Ingram, one of the authors of *The Degree Generation*, this narrow focus on social mobility is not, and cannot be, the solution to class inequality. Indeed, as Ingram and Sol Gamsu (2002), have recently pointed out, discussions about the relationship between graduate employers and inequality must engage with the work professionals *do*, as well as *who they are*. Here, they point to the paradox that the employers taking class most seriously *internally* are arguably the same ones accentuating class inequalities in the work they do *externally*. Similarly, as Louise Ashley has noted, many professional employers are directly implicated in driving the kind of high pay that has contributed so profoundly to growing income inequality in many Western countries.

In this way, Ashley has gone on to argue, it is important to recognize that organizational social mobility agendas often act as a form of cultural legitimation, allowing professional employers to align themselves with egalitarian values while obscuring their role in perpetuating class inequalities in society more broadly. This blind spot in government and organizational social mobility agendas was a source of much frustration to me when I sat on the UK government's Social Mobility Commission between 2018 and

2021. While on the commission, I repeatedly argued for a broader 'class agenda' among professional employers that focused not only on social mobility, but also, more broadly, on class or socio-economic inequality. Yet, as only one of 12 commissioners, and as someone lacking the rhetorical skill to win over their hearts and minds (and perhaps the appetite to be a truly confrontational figure), I was largely unsuccessful in making this case.

My hope, though, is that forceful books like this can provide the kind of evidence-base we need to continue to advocate for more radical policy goals. Concretely, I would suggest that a realizable policy aim may be the enactment of the 'Socioeconomic Duty' contained within the Equality Act 2010. This section both speaks to equality of opportunity in making class origin a protected characteristic (meaning it would be against the law to discriminate against someone on the basis of class origin), but also goes significantly further, requiring government and all public bodies to have due regard for reducing inequalities of outcome, especially as they relate to socio-economic disadvantage. While successive governments have declined to bring this section into effect, perhaps it is high time that graduate employers stepped in to fill the gap.

Reference
Ingram, N. and Gamsu, S. (2022) Talking the talk of social mobility: the political performance of a misguided agenda, *Sociological Research Online*, https://doi.org/10.1177/13607804211055493

1

Graduate Success and Graduate Lives

Introduction

This book is about the workings of social class, race (specifically whiteness) and gender in young graduates' lives. Its aim is to provide insights into the ways in which the dominant policy goals of social mobility and graduate employability are experienced by young people themselves. The book is based on a longitudinal study of young people from working-class and middle-class backgrounds (the Paired Peers project), who attended one of two universities in Bristol, UK, during the 2010s: the University of the West of England Bristol (UWE), a modern 'post-92' university; and the University of Bristol (UoB), a member of the high-status Russell Group[1] of universities. The book traces the unfolding of their

---

[1] The Russell Group is a self-styled group of 24 'leading' universities in the UK, including Oxbridge, which have distinguished themselves from the rest in order to position themselves for market advantage in a highly stratified system. Membership is not necessarily a marker of quality, as some Russell Group universities have performance ratings that are lower than universities outside of the grouping, but membership carries significant status within the UK system. Their naming as the 'Russell Group' is reputed to have sprung from the fact that the initial meetings to discuss the grouping happened in the Russell Hotel in Bloomsbury, London.

young graduate lives through an analysis of a unique longitudinal qualitative data set gathered over a seven-year period. This is the second of two books from the project team. The first book (Bathmaker et al, 2016) presents the findings of the first phase of the project and considers students' experiences of getting in, getting on and getting out of university. It demonstrates the significance of social class, as well as gender and race, for students' experience of higher education and contributes a critical and complex understanding of social reproduction and social mobility through higher education. In this follow-on book, we use data from both Phase 2 and Phase 1 of the project, and turn the spotlight onto the transition beyond university through to four years post-graduation. Most data about graduates in the UK are collected through the national graduate outcomes survey, a limited quantitative survey that captures a snapshot of graduate destinations just 15 months after leaving university. Our book provides an original qualitative longitudinal perspective on the process of early career development, which is not captured by the graduate outcomes survey or by other studies.

The Paired Peers project (2010–17) followed a cohort of 90 young people from middle-class and working-class backgrounds who started undergraduate study in England in 2010 and who graduated in 2013/14. The study followed these young people throughout their undergraduate lives and for four years post-graduation. The participants were interviewed ten times over this seven-year period. Whereas much research on graduate success focuses on employment status and/or salary at a defined point shortly after graduation, our study is able to take a longitudinal view on employment destinations and respond to the limitations of data that merely capture first employment (Sage et al, 2013) or employment at a single point not long after graduation (Hoare and Corver, 2010). We are therefore able to consider both the complexity of the transition process and the significance of time and space in the making of lives. The central arguments of the book hang on a theoretical framework that considers the significance of the process of transition over a prolonged period of time; specifically, we examine the forms of capital that have been acquired throughout our participants' lives, the capital they accumulate in the transition from higher education to work and, most importantly, the ways in which they convert these various capitals into symbolic capital. The focus on symbolic capital provides an original lens with which to understand the makings of advantage and disadvantage on the graduate labour market.

In this chapter, we begin by considering dominant framings of graduate 'success', how this is viewed and measured by multiple higher education actors, and what is missing from broader conceptualizations and measurements of graduate progression. We lay out the context within which young people progressed from university to graduate lives in the 2010s through a broad overview of graduate outcomes within the context of the higher education policy landscape in the UK. Within this context, we then unpack ideas around social mobility and the role of higher education in supporting government mobility goals, drawing links to graduates' own dreams and aspirations, as well as the reality of the labour market. The chapter then gives an overview of the theoretical approach to the analysis in this book, outlining the Bourdieusian concept of social magic, Berlant's concept of 'cruel optimism' and Tholen's concept of symbolic closure, all of which are utilized and developed in the chapters that follow. The chapter ends with a summary of the chapters in the book.

Constructions of graduate success

There are many different ways of 'being a graduate', and this book is testament to some of the diversity in experiences of transition from higher education. The term 'graduate' is laden with particular social meanings and often conjures up notions of narrowly defined career success in the social imagination. Indeed, in the UK, the concept of 'graduate success' is realized through the social construction of the 'graduate job' and the 'graduate labour market'. The contemporary graduate, therefore, is brought into being and made concrete through policy frameworks (such as the Teaching Excellence and Student Outcomes Framework [TEF]) and measurement tools (such as the Destination of Leavers from Higher Education [DLHE] and Graduate Outcomes surveys), with their emphasis on narrowly circumscribed success. This works to create a myth of acceptable and normative pathways against which higher education leavers define their own transitions. As Christie (2019: 331) argues: 'the figure of "the Graduate" is a powerful symbolic figure against which individuals author themselves. Being a graduate has both material and symbolic implications that vary depending on subject studied and university attended'.

In this book, we challenge the myth of acceptable ways to be a graduate and argue for recognition of individual graduates' values and the meanings they attach to their own lives and transitions as they exit higher education, while recognizing the importance of securing work that enables graduates to lead the lives they would wish to live. In doing so, we recognize the need for a shift in higher education discourse to enable the valuing of multiple forms of success (Houghton, 2019). Normative discourses around both aspirations and transitions form a doxic order (Bourdieu, 1977; Bourdieu and Eagleton, 1992) that involves a self-evident expectation of what being a graduate should involve and perpetuates inequality by narrowing the frame of what counts as acceptable forms of success (Wallace, 2019). This book challenges the doxic order by exploring 'success' pathways that do not necessarily adhere to the typical graduate success script, with its unquestioned principles (Morrin, 2015). The longitudinal nature of the study affords the opportunity to think carefully about different pathways that students might take on their journey to find work that is meaningful to them. This enables us to provide an analysis that recognizes the importance of the unfolding *process* of developing a career path, rather than fixing the achievement of a graduate career at a *defined outcome* point.

Most discussions of being a contemporary graduate focus on the material factors of employment type and salary, assuming a neat and linear transition from education to graduate employment. Research by Purcell et al (2013), however, shows that between 1999 and 2009, the percentage of graduates in what they define as 'non-graduate employment' 30 months after graduation doubled from 20 to 40 per cent, and more recent data from the UK's Higher Education Statistical Agency (HESA, 2021) show that in 2018/19, 31 per cent of graduates were not in 'high-skilled work'. This means that around one third of graduates are failing to achieve the markers of success in the way most widely accepted by societal discourses and expected by higher education policy makers, such as the Office for Students (OfS), which defines graduates as being in highly skilled or professional roles. Such a reductive reading of graduates as attached to certain sections of the labour market encourages a narrow understanding of success as something concrete and measurable (associated with highly skilled and 'professional' work); this renders the 31 per cent of recent graduates who are not in this type of employment as failures. Subsequently, the 'symbolic implications' of what it means to be a graduate, as identified by Christie, are often overlooked, including the value individuals attribute to themselves. This opens up questions about the construction of the graduate and graduate success within policy and popular discourse.

While there is a significant amount of research on the construction of the higher education 'student' (Brooks, 2018a, 2018b, 2019; Brooks and Abrahams, 2020), there is very little on the construction of 'the graduate'. In the chapters that follow, we consider both the material and the symbolic implications of being a graduate, and unpack the notion of graduate success, through an exploration of different graduates' life and labour market transitions and experiences. In doing so, we provide a more expansive view of success, recognizing that success means different things to different people and that ideas of success shift over time in the years that follow graduation. In short, we consider the making of graduate lives that go beyond making a living.

In doing so, we also recognize the importance that students and graduates themselves attach to labour market success, and consider their framing of graduate work. Tomlinson's (2008) study of students' perceptions of graduate work shows that the discourse of the 'graduate as higher earner' prevails as a trickle-down outcome of policy messages. However, he demonstrates that the students in his study were also developing an increasing awareness of the need for 'credential distinction' (Tomlinson, 2008: 56), which effectively meant a consideration of the status of the degree-awarding institution in the graduate labour market. In Tomlinson's (2008: 58) study, awareness of the importance of different forms of capital fuelled the notion that a degree was not enough or that it was only 'half the story', and his participants developed awareness of the need to develop additional value through, for example, extra-curricular experiences. The Paired Peers research builds upon this and shows how the discourse of 'a degree is not enough' has taken hold in the social imaginary of the contemporary higher education student, an argument that we developed in our first book (Bathmaker et al, 2016). This showed the intensification of capital-accumulation activities among contemporary students from all class backgrounds, as well as what we have referred to as middle-class students' 'hyper-mobilization' of such capital. This current book considers how multiple forms of capital come into play in the process of graduate labour market transitions in a context of diminished opportunity.

It is now a taken-for-granted assumption that the graduate labour market is tough, congested and highly competitive. However, students are not all equally equipped to recognize this and play the game of preparing for it (Bathmaker et al, 2013), and forms of capital other than a degree certificate are increasingly important (Burke, 2016). In considering how inequalities play out in students' own understandings of higher education and labour market success, Burke et al (2019: 1713) argue that 'anachronistic conceptions of the graduate labour market' can lead working-class or non-traditional students to focus solely on building capital through academic knowledge and credentials. In their study of students' perceptions of graduate employment, they offer a typology of the graduate labour market aligned to the type of institution attended. Students attending modern universities (those that gained university status following the Further and Higher Education Act 1992 in the UK, often referred to as 'post-92' universities) are more likely to have a 'naïve' understanding, whereby they consider the relationship between degree and employment as linear, while students attending the high-status Russell Group of universities are more likely to express a 'knowing' (Burke et al, 2019: 1715, 1716) orientation that recognizes the need for additional forms of capital gained through extra-curricular experiences. They present these as classed differences, where 'post-92' stands as a proxy for working-class and 'Russell Group' as a proxy for middle-class students, though they do not look at the complexity of the class make-up of students at each of the universities in their study. In Phase 1 of the Paired Peers project, we found a more complex picture of orientations to developing forms of capital in preparation for success on the graduate labour market. These were less to do with institution attended and more to do with social class background. We found that the middle-class students at both post-92 and Russell Group universities in our research project were savvy about acquiring and mobilizing capitals through extra-curricular activities and internships (Bathmaker et al, 2013), whereas some working-class students started to recognize how to 'play the game' only as they came closer to the end of their degree study (Bathmaker et al, 2016). In the current book, which draws on this unique longitudinal study of graduates from working-class and middle-class backgrounds, we contribute a more in-depth understanding of the process of developing capitals, tracing *how* capitals are accumulated and developed over time, based on a seven-year view of the experiences of young people as they move through student and graduate transitions and experiences. We are able to explore in a complex and nuanced way both the *accumulation* and the *deployment* of capitals by these young people, as well as their transitions towards a 'successful' graduate life.

Moreover, the longitudinal nature of the Paired Peers project allows us to provide a bigger picture of people's perceptions and orientations, meaning that we can move beyond a story told about oneself at one particular moment. As argued by Holland and Thomson (2009: 453): '[an] accumulation of narratives of self may provide a route to move beyond the life as told to gain insight into the life as lived as well as other possible unlived lives that fall away'. The narratives gathered for the Paired Peers project afford the opportunity to interrogate and critique the normative discourses of social mobility and aspiration in relation to graduates' perceptions of their own successes and failures over time. Our extensive and rich data set allows us to think deeply about the assumed link between education and social mobility – another key discourse in constructions of graduate success. This is something we turn to later in the chapter, but we first present an overview of the UK higher education policy context as a framing for the Paired Peers project.

Graduate outcomes and employability within the UK higher education policy landscape

The percentage of the UK population classified as a graduate rose significantly from 17 per cent in 1992 to 38 per cent in 2013 (ONS, 2013), the year in which the cohort in this study graduated. Indeed, this rise, which is considered to represent the *massification* of higher education, has resulted in an important generational shift in degree qualification status for the millennial cohort (Finn et al, 2021),[2] who are now widely regarded in the academic literature as 'the degree generation' (Bathmaker et al, 2016). However, at the same time as the rise in higher education participation and graduation, the returns to higher education (understood as the increased earnings linked to higher education study) have been diminishing (Boero et al, 2019). In a comparison of data from different birth cohorts, Boero et al show that the millennial cohort of graduates at age 25 earn 11 per cent more than their non-graduate counterparts but that this compares negatively with the previous generation (Generation X) of graduates, who earned 19 per cent more than their non-graduate peers. Contemporary graduates now face both substantial underemployment and a struggle to find work that utilizes their knowledge and skills, and this continues to disproportionately affect those from working-class backgrounds (Elias et al, 2021). Alongside these diminishing returns and the parallel expansion of initial participation rates (participation rates for 17- to 30-year-old first-time participants in England) to 47 per cent by 2010 (DBIS, 2011), the financial cost of participation in higher education in England has shifted from the state to students with the introduction of tuition fees in 1999. This burden continues to grow with decreases in the loan repayment salary threshold and planned increases in interest rates in line with rising inflation. The Paired Peers graduates entered higher education in 2010 at a point when the tuition fees paid by students were capped at £3,000 per annum, in line with the Higher Education Act 2004. They started their undergraduate study in the same year that the Browne Review (Browne, 2010) was published, which paved the way for an increase of tuition fees of up to £9,000 per annum for students commencing study in the 2012–13 academic year.

With the shift away from free tuition, a discourse of 'students as consumers' has developed that has ultimately led to an increased focus on graduate employment, as consumer satisfaction is

---

[2] The millennial cohort constitutes those born between 1981 and 1996. The graduates in our study were born in the middle of this range. Generation X is the generation before the millennial cohort, those born between 1965 and 1980.

predicated on value for money and measured by employment outcomes, rather than by knowledge gained. The contemporary higher education student has been encouraged to enact a consumer relationship with a university system that appears to promise enhanced employment outcomes as part of an unwritten contract (Bathmaker and Bowl, 2018; Bowl et al, 2018) but, at the same time, is unfairly critiqued for their behaviour (Finn et al, 2021). Notably, tuition fees paid for by students have been justified on the grounds that higher education qualifications lead to increased earning power via graduate employment (see, for example, Browne, 2010; DfES, 2003). This provides good grounds for students to expect their degree to facilitate employment success and for government to be reactive to signs of labour market struggle. A perhaps inevitable outcome of these shifts from the state to the individual in financing higher education has been the development of the problematic notion of 'value-for-money degrees' and their corollary of 'low-value degrees', both of which terms are increasingly deployed by the UK's OfS and the Department for Education. The value of a degree is becoming narrowly defined in policy discourses by employment outcomes and earnings. This move has a negative differential impact on post-92 and newer universities, who recruit larger proportions of working-class students, and on universities located in the north of England and Wales, whose graduates earn less than those based in London and the south of England (OfS, 2021). This is at a time when the increase in earning power traditionally enjoyed by university graduates has been diminishing, while fees have been rising (Finn et al, 2021), and evidence continues to show a class pay gap in terms of employment outcomes (Friedman et al, 2017). Despite this, the *expected* increase in earning power for graduates (regardless of the constrained reality) continues to impact upon higher education policies, with graduate outcomes operating as a key policy lever and a mechanism for holding higher education institutions to account for employment destinations.

Graduate labour market outcomes have become a key measurement in determining how universities are positioned in national and global rankings, including the TEF in the UK and the Quacquarelli Symonds (QS) World University Rankings. The resulting league tables of universities that stem from these exercises do not take into account the significant inequalities both among and within different national higher education systems and labour markets, but simply present employment destinations as a sign of university quality. In the UK, for example, the implementation of the TEF to English higher education institutions in 2016 heralded an increase in focus on graduate outcomes, as employment destinations (measured through the DLHE) became a key quality metric. Since its introduction into policy discussions in 2015, the 'Teaching Excellence Framework' has been rebranded as the 'Teaching Excellence and Student Outcomes Framework' (Business, Innovation and Skills Committee, 2016). Initially, the TEF measures were benchmarked against the university's expected performance (which included recognition of the student intake across such measures as academic performance and social background), but this proved to be highly controversial when the first ratings were published (especially with some Russell Group universities who fared badly using this benchmarked system). Consequently, TEF judgements are now made on a combination of benchmarked and absolute measures. The TEF has become a key assessment tool of higher education quality across the four nations of the UK, and graduate employment outcomes have become 'a key element in the inter-institutional competition that characterises an increasingly marketised sector' (Morrison, 2019: 31). Through the TEF rankings exercise, incorporating these assessments of graduate employment outcomes, UK universities receive gold, silver or bronze awards, which then operate as a consumer-facing mark of quality. As a result, universities have become caught up in an employability game, whereby they attempt to affect graduate outcomes in order to boost their position in national league tables.

Many universities have adopted an approach to enhancing employability that places the emphasis on developing individual skills and attributes (Burke and Christie, 2019), with university departments held to account for their students' performance in the Graduate Outcomes survey and its impact on TEF awards. There is an institutional-level assumption that enhancing employability through the development of skills will itself lead to better results, perhaps because tackling the underlying structural causes of social inequality and labour market opportunity is a task beyond the control of the education sector. A number of different approaches are now used to develop individuals' skills. The work of Tomlinson

(2017), for example, advocates for increased understandings of the sorts of capital that graduates need to enhance employability. This goes beyond developing additional skills to consider the importance of forms of social and cultural capital, such as building networks and engaging in valued forms of work experience. However, the problem with an approach based on enhancing employability at the individual level is that structural issues are regularly denied, or at least obscured (Moreau and Leathwood, 2006). There is a failure to take account of a myriad of important factors that impact on inequalities in access to employment, such as race, ethnicity, social class, gender, disability, regional disparities in relation to opportunity and institution attended. All these factors affect how different capitals are read, recognized and misrecognized by employers (Rivera, 2012, 2015; Ingram and Allen, 2019). Further, these approaches do not routinely consider and seek to address how structural inequalities are internalized and generate classed, gendered and racialized forms of embodied capital that are misrecognized as 'other' by employers. This book addresses ideas about employability, embodied capital, labour market experiences and outcomes, exploring how advantage and disadvantage play out in the processes of graduate career development. Our intention is to highlight how employability support for disadvantaged students needs to take account of the structural conditions that affect the hopes, aspirations and opportunities of individual students in different ways. The next section considers how an emphasis on individual aspiration has problematically become central to discourses of graduate success, social mobility and achieving equality in the UK.

Aspirations and social mobility: bright futures and broken dreams

Since 2010, a rise has been seen in the framing of aspiration as the solution to educational and social inequalities within the UK, as well as in other Western democracies globally. It has 'become an enduring trope across the discursive landscape of successive UK governments' (Allen, 2014: 760). Despite significant evidence that aspiration in young people is not lacking and that increasing it is not likely to solve the problems caused by poverty, it remains a key feature of policy relating to education and employment outcomes in the 2020s. The discourse of aspiration is tied up with the discourse of social mobility, and higher education is proffered as the vehicle for increasing both.

Despite the loosening of 'the relationship between graduate jobs, skills, careers and rewards in western economies' (Tholen, 2017a: 1071), social mobility remains a dominant policy goal. Within this frame, higher education is regarded as being a key driver of mobility. In the UK, this idea has been fostered by a series of reports from the Social Mobility Commission that point to the key role of universities in upward social mobility and elite formation (Milburn, 2009, 2012a, 2012b; Social Mobility Commission, 2019, 2020). Accordingly, government targets for increasing participation in higher education have been set over successive decades (DES, 1991; Public Accounts Committee, 2009; Boliver, 2011; DBIS 2016) and have been integral to the shift in participation from 35 to over 50 per cent in the last 20 years. More recently, however, government commitment to increasing higher education participation has waned and higher education has instead come under attack for its failure to deliver job opportunities and social mobility. For example, Michelle Donelan MP, former UK Minister for Higher Education (2021–22), called for 'true' social mobility, which 'is about getting people to choose the path that will lead to their desired destination and enabling them to complete that path' (Donelan, 2020). Donelan's solution to the severed link between higher education and social mobility is to promote the idea that working-class young people should consider alternative pathways to employment, which, as Ingram and Gamsu (2022: 4) argue, 'promulgates a "stay in your lane" approach to higher education and betrays an ideology that is underpinned by social reproduction, where working-class kids are encouraged to aspire to "working-class jobs"'. It is within this rhetorical context of aspiration and social mobility that the graduates in our study have navigated the post-university labour market. They have emerged from university with more debt than previous generations and from an education system that expects (indeed demands) higher aspirations into a labour market that is largely unable to deliver the outcomes that match the latter (Tholen and Brown, 2017). Universities have therefore become, in policy terms, both the vehicles of social mobility and the sites of its failure. The recognition of this faltering of the social mobility promise of higher education has shifted attention from widening access and participation to curtailing the graduate pool through the expansion of both further education and non-graduate routes to employment, as well as new apprenticeship pathways. These are becoming framed as the new sites tasked with delivering social mobility (Bathmaker, 2018). Instead of thinking about the barriers to social mobility in terms of the availability of labour market opportunities, the education system is scrutinized and becomes the locus of a solution that it cannot deliver.

It is no coincidence that political appetite for increasing young people's participation in higher education has dwindled since the early 2010s. The increase in graduates from both middle-class and working-class backgrounds in higher education has led to increased competition for graduate jobs, and university is no longer a guaranteed middle-class route to secure professional employment or, indeed, social mobility. Alongside the increase in university students over recent decades, the supply of graduate-level jobs has been decreasing (Brown, 2003; Brown et al, 2011) and the financial returns to education have been diminishing (Goldthorpe, 2016). Brown (2003) uses the term 'opportunity trap' to characterize how families' and young people's investment in university education as a guarantee of securing graduate work does not necessarily deliver. As a significant proportion of graduates never succeed in achieving this type of work, higher education can be seen to generate both broken promises and broken dreams. Young people are promised bright futures by the conflation of higher education and social mobility, despite a significant body of evidence showing that these are not always realizable. As Ingram and Gamsu (2022: 4–5) argue, 'the promotion of the achievability of social mobility, and by discursive association, "a good life", allows government to distract attention from the lack of real opportunity for labour market reward, and mobility for all', which highlights that it is easier to claim an allegiance to the ideals of social mobility than to tackle sources of inequality.

Being a graduate no longer axiomatically entails social mobility, and in many ways, old class structures of reproduction are maintained through higher education and play out on the graduate labour market, leaving significant numbers of graduates (especially those from the working class and minority ethnic groups) with broken dreams instead of upward mobility experiences. The term 'cruel optimism' (Berlant, 2011) fittingly conveys the process of raised hopes and the way they may be blighted. Berlant (2011) argues that we cling to unachievable promises of the good life, achieved through hard work, while the realities of neoliberal capitalist economies deny many of us the opportunities to achieve them. It is a 'vital attachment to the fantasy of the "good life" (including the promise of upward mobility, happiness and economic security)' (Mendick et al, 2018: 9), despite the erosion of the structures that might enable the realization of these dreams.

Conceptualizing decision making and future planning

In this book, we explore the decision-making processes involved in seeking to achieve a 'bright future' as situated and ongoing occurrences. By this, we mean that we recognize decision making as a complex interplay of structure and agency, with habitus (the internalization of structure that informs agency) as the guiding principle, rather than as a one-off moment of choice. We therefore consider the unfolding of young adults' lives as a process or a series of 'happenings' or experiences that orientate them towards what might be construed as a fateful outcome. This connects with, but moves beyond, Giddens' (1991: 113) notion of 'fateful moments': 'Fateful moments are times when events come together in such a way that an individual stands, as it were, at a crossroads in his existence; or where a person learns of information with fateful consequences.' While Giddens conceptualizes fate as a time for agency at key points in existence where a person encounters moments of critical decision making, we consider fate as an ongoing and everyday process in which outcomes are a result of continuous responses to the world as it presents itself.

We also engage with the idea of 'critical moments' in young people's transitions (Holland and Thomson, 2009) as a fruitful way of thinking about key junctures and events that steer the direction of the life course. Holland and Thomson (2009: 455) define a critical moment as 'An event described in an interview that the interviewee or the researcher, or both, understood as having important consequences for the young person's life and identity.' While the idea of a critical moment leading to a crossroads where key decisions need to be made is compelling, we were also curious to explore what happens when there is no significant critical moment, yet material circumstances, a history of experiences and dispositions elide to orientate a person in a direction that then has a fateful outcome. In doing this, we asked questions about decision making and choices – or, more often, non-decision making and non-choices. We think about the ways in which a subjective rationality in decision making might be boundaried (Goldthorpe, 2007; Glaesser and Cooper, 2013) and place emphasis on the process of decision making through *being*, rather than through *choosing*. Our approach connects with that of Hodkinson and Sparkes (1997: 41), who consider periods of routine to be integral to decision-making processes:

> Within a field, people make pragmatically rational decisions within their culturally-derived horizons for action, at turning-points. These turning-points are both preceded and followed by periods of routine, which themselves are located within the field and the macro-context. The periods of routine and the turning-points are themselves inter-related, so that neither can be understood fully without the other, and the separation between them is often arbitrary. The pathway from turning-point to turning-point can be predictable and smooth or irregular and idiosyncratic.

Our theoretical perspective throughout the book is Bourdieusian, even when we do not directly utilize his concepts. In the case of considering choice and decision making as routine, everyday and boundaried, we align with Bourdieu's concepts of habitus and field. The habitus, as the internalization of structure, generates ways of being and acting. These practices take place within a social field, which, in turn, impacts upon the parameters for action. In this way, practices, decision making, conceptions of the possible, aspirations and strategies are derived from the interaction between habitus and field, and are therefore neither fully determined nor fully willed (Bourdieu, 2000, 2002). Our particular contribution to thinking about graduate labour market transitions is through our detailed explorations of the processes involved not only in the accumulation of capitals, but also in the conversion of capitals over time, that is, the conversion of one form of capital into another (for example, the conversion of economic capital into cultural capital, which can then be utilized to build social capital, which, in turn, might lead to employment and ultimately further economic capital). Much research that uses a Bourdieusian lens considers discrete stocks and combinations of social, cultural and economic capital, and their correlation with advantage and disadvantage. In this book, we pay particular attention to the capital conversion process and therefore uniquely explicate the ways in which capital becomes useful and mobilized for advantage. In doing this, we contribute to understandings of symbolic capital, which is underutilized in empirical studies of educational transitions. Bourdieu (1989: 17) defines symbolic capital as 'the form that the various species of capital assume when they are perceived and recognized as legitimate', and it is this recognition of legitimacy that facilitates the convertibility of capitals.

We highlight the increasing importance of symbolic recognition in the conversion of capitals in contexts of increased higher education participation and reduced (or congested) graduate labour market opportunity, showing how it is the construction of value, rather than the accumulation of capitals per se, that generates graduate distinction and leads to further advantaging the already privileged. Our focus on the process of converting valued capitals by graduates to enable them to succeed suggests that opening up the advantages enjoyed by the successful middle classes to others is much more than a matter of increasing the stocks of capital available to those from working-class backgrounds. In the book, we use the idea of social magic to draw out how both structural and symbolic inequalities in the narratives of our participants are obscured and remain hidden from view through processes of what Bourdieu (1990: 129) terms 'social alchemy'.

Symbolic recognition and conversion of capitals on the labour market

As already noted in this chapter, the congested graduate labour market demands that graduates mobilize other forms of capital in order to gain positional advantage (Bathmaker et al, 2016; Tholen, 2017b). In Bourdieusian terms, these forms of capital take three forms: economic, cultural and social (Bourdieu, 1986). Economic capital denotes material wealth and financial resources, and social capital denotes valuable networks and connections. Cultural capital, according to Bourdieu (1986), takes three different forms: embodied cultural capital (embodied practices and dispositions); objectified cultural capital (cultural goods, such as books, clothes and artwork); and institutionalized cultural capital (for example, credentials and qualifications). These forms of capital are interlaced in the analysis presented in the chapters in this book. Our particular contribution is to consider the role of symbolic capital and symbolic recognition in the generation of labour market inequalities. Bourdieu (1986: 18) explains how cultural capital connects to symbolic capital: 'Because the social conditions of its transmission and acquisition are more disguised than those of economic capital, it is predisposed to function as symbolic capital, i.e., to be unrecognised as capital and recognised as legitimate competence, as authority exerting an effect of (mis)recognition.' It is this idea of recognition and misrecognition of different forms of embodied capital that is explored further in this book, going beyond ideas of capital accumulation and mobilization to consider how symbolic classifications operate to render certain capitals as carrying more latent and transmissible value. Tholen (2017a) argues for the significance of 'symbolic' closure in graduate labour market outcomes. Here, he builds on the concept of social closure, whereby social groups monopolize resources and exclude others from them, to consider how social domination by the privileged is generated through the symbolic realm, rather than merely through control of material resources. He argues that 'the reliance on exclusion through categorisation and classification, becomes of greater importance in a graduate labour market that no longer offers any clarity about what graduate skills, jobs and rewards constitute and signify' (Tholen, 2017a: 1067). This represents 'symbolic closure', a means of legitimating certain graduates and their cultural capital, and excluding others and their cultural capital. Embodied cultural capital is of particular significance to this process, as the body is a key site for conveying value. Following this view, the classification of the value of forms of embodied cultural capital is vital to understanding how inequalities play out in the processes of labour market transition. This is key for going beyond the narrower understandings of graduates' transitions and successes highlighted earlier.

Along with the notion of symbolic closure, we utilize the concept of social magic, or social alchemy, to think about the hidden processes at work in the transition from university to graduate employment. Bourdieu (1990: 129) proposes that: 'The transformation of any kind of capital into symbolic capital, a legitimate possession grounded in the nature of its possessor, is the fundamental operation of social alchemy.' Not only do we highlight the importance of understanding transition as *process* to gain important insights into outcomes, but we also highlight the significance of the conversion of acquired stocks of economic, cultural and social capital into symbolic capital. Our analysis emphasizes the social magic, or social alchemy, at play in this conversion, which entails the necessary obfuscation of the nature of the exchange to present the outcome as fair, legitimate and objective.

The role of symbolic capital is often overlooked in discussions of higher education and graduate employment, which more often focus on the economic–social–cultural capital triad (Burke, 2016). However, shedding light on the capital conversion or mobilization process (Bathmaker et al, 2013) demonstrates the need for capitals to be recognized and legitimated in order to function as a resource. This exposes the complexities of the way differing forms of capital achieve recognition and, therefore, power. As Bourdieu (1989: 23) explains:

> symbolic power has to be based on the possession of symbolic capital. The power to impose upon other minds a vision, old or new, of social divisions depends on the social authority acquired in previous struggles. Symbolic capital is a credit; it is the power granted to those who have obtained sufficient recognition to be in a position to impose recognition.

Working within this framework, we build on the work of Ingram and Allen (2019), who develop Bourdieu's lesser-known concept of social magic to account for processes of capital legitimation in elite graduate recruitment. They use as an example the role of graduate employers in 'reading' the capital of prospective employees, and imposing recognition and value. They develop a theory of social magic to explain how certain attributes and forms of expression (predominantly possessed and embodied by the privileged classes) are bestowed with value and recognition, whereas other forms of capital (predominately possessed and embodied by the dominated classes) are overlooked and misrecognized. For Ingram and Allen (2019: 737), social magic is the:

> means of theorising the capital conversion process, and goes beyond Bourdieu's thinking about the forms of capital to unpack the process of value exchange. It is through social magic that the cultural arbitrary becomes disguised, and cultural forms of capital are endowed with symbolic recognition. This conversion allows (and is necessary for) the legitimation of privilege.

Threadgold (2020: 34), drawing on the work of Ingram and Allen, highlights both the 'magical rewards' for the privileged and the obfuscation of the social struggles that have given rise to the current order of things:

> We ignore 'how the way things are' emerges from social struggles over time that have advantaged some groups or individuals more than others, and how that socially formulated order magically rewards some people, seemingly naturally, when really they are lucky to be born into the right place in social space.

Capital, therefore, is not necessarily a material resource or quality that can be straightforwardly acquired, learned or built, but rather embodied and becomes real only in the conversion process when value is bestowed on some bodily performances and denied to others. This understanding of the ways in which capitals work recognizes the locus of graduate 'unemployability' to be not the graduates themselves, but the unequal structures of the social field in which they operate, including the hierarchical higher education system, unequal labour markets and employers' recruitment processes. Social magic allows for a Bourdieusian analysis that attends to the legitimation of the symbolic power of the privileged through processes of capital conversion that leave the very workings of privilege largely hidden: 'Social magic is the means of obscuring the conditions in which value is constructed so that fit comes to be seen as "natural" and the cultural arbitrary is denied. It is a useful concept for considering how value is both constructed and mobilised (as capital)' (Ingram and Allen, 2019: 729). We therefore consider not only the capitals that graduates bring with them to the field of the graduate labour market, but also how these capitals are mobilized, recognized and exchanged. This is important for understanding the ways in which advantage and discrimination are engendered through the recognition and misrecognition of the capitals that graduates from different backgrounds possess. It also helps us to unpack the ways in which forms of capital come to be seen as the naturalized qualities of those possessing them, rather than unfair advantages. This is part of the process of what Tholen (2017a, 2017b) has usefully coined 'symbolic closure'.

This conceptual lens directs the analysis towards a focus on the practices, dispositions and orientations of sets of individuals, and in what follows, we offer in-depth presentations of a limited number of cases in each chapter. This allows us to explore the ways in which capital is accrued and exchanged, and to detail the process of symbolic closure and social magic. While this approach relies on an analysis at the level of the individual, it is worth remembering that a Bourdieusian framework regards individual practice as emanating from the internalization of structure. Our analysis therefore reflects a consideration of the structural conditions of the social fields of the education system and the labour market, including the power dynamics of class, race and gender in shaping social practices and, ultimately, labour market outcomes. Our data set is unique. As Chapter 2 explains, we generated a rich qualitative data set over a seven-year period that allows us to provide original insights into the micro-processes of transitions from university to graduate life. This enables us to highlight the ways in which class, race and gender shape transitions. However, our data do not allow us to offer the type of analysis that statistical data can provide, which are able to show large-scale quantitative patterns of inequality. Where relevant, we draw on statistics and such quantitative studies as Futuretrack (Elias et al, 2021) to highlight these patterns. Building on the evidence provided by these studies, our work has the specific aim of providing an original contribution to understanding how the inequalities of class, race and gender that they identify are produced and reproduced in everyday situated practices.

Overview of the chapters in the book

The key arguments that connect the chapters relate to our theoretical contribution to the field of graduate employment, with our specific focus on how capitals are converted into symbolic capital through a process of social magic, which, in turn, facilitates symbolic and, ultimately, social closure. We draw these arguments out in different ways in each of the chapters and bring them together in our final discussion in the conclusion of the book. A brief synopsis of each chapter and its theoretical framing is introduced in the following.

Chapter 2: Moving on Up: Researching the Lives and Careers of Young Graduates

Chapter 2 provides an overview of the project design and an explanation of the methods that were employed in Phase 2. It provides demographic details about the participants, including social class, university attended and gender. The chapter discusses measures of social class, the limitations of definitions of gender and the operationalization of the concepts of 'race' and ethnicity. This includes a discussion of whiteness and an acknowledgement of the racially skewed nature of the sample. The chapter ends with an outline of the methodological approach.

Chapter 3: London Calling: Being Mobile and Mobilizing Capitals

Chapter 3 takes as its focus London and its role in the reproduction of inequality through the perpetuation of discourses that problematically conflate social and geographical mobility. While London is widely recognized as a hub for elite graduate recruiters, particularly in respect to jobs in finance, law and information technology (IT), and a place that has seen a disproportionate growth in professional and managerial positions in comparison to the rest of Great Britain, it requires the mobilization of elite forms of social, cultural and economic capital. Moreover, moving to, or living in, London is seen as an obvious next step for graduates with high aspirations, without any recognition of the privilege required to facilitate such aspirations and opportunities for mobility. The chapter explores these issues by considering how proximity and access to London itself operates as a form of capital but that this is not enough to ensure success. We highlight the importance of embodied forms of cultural capital that are recognized as cosmopolitanism and argue that through processes of social magic, these bodily displays read as competence in the 'elite metropolitan vortex' of London (Cunningham and Savage, 2015).

Chapter 4: 'There's No Place Like Home': Graduate Mobilities and Spatial Belonging

Chapter 4 expands the discussion of mobility to explore the significance of 'home' for graduate mobility. It considers the ways in which home contributes to capacities to navigate graduate futures and explores the legitimation of certain forms of geographical navigation over others. For young people who participate in higher education in England, the dominant narrative is one of leaving behind the family home and becoming geographically mobile in terms of both the 'student experience' and graduate life. The chapter problematizes the way in which geographical mobility – leaving the home place – is recognized as success by exploring both the cost of mobility and the value of choosing to stay, with a focus on working-class and middle-class capitals and orientations to home. The chapter questions the legitimization of 'being geographically mobile' as a valued form of capital and, in doing so, shows the significance of home and locality as a potential form of valuable but misrecognized social and cultural capital for working-class graduates.

Chapter 5: Jobs for the Boys? Gender, Capital and Male-Dominated Fields

Chapter 5 considers the working of gender in male-dominated fields and the ways in which this plays out for men and women on the graduate labour market, focusing on the field of engineering.

The chapter draws on Bourdieu's concept of symbolic violence to expose embodied gendered experiences of the workplace that delegitimize women's position and value. Contrasting narratives of two successful graduates from the UoB, one male and one female, are used to show how stocks of relevant and valued capitals are not sufficient to make a career in engineering, where the working of gender means that men are able to readily fit in and progress, while women are out-of-place invaders in a male-dominated space. The chapter shows the ways in which forms of (white, middle-class, masculine) embodied cultural capital can be more readily converted in a field that has been constructed to recognize its value.

Chapter 6: Intersections of Class and Gender in the Making of 'Top Boys' in the Finance Sector

Chapter 6 considers the intersection of class and gender in the making of 'top boys', focusing on the finance sector. The chapter highlights key class-based differences in the way in which aspirations for success play out, based on the narratives of three young men from different social class locations. Comparing these narratives highlights the making of contemporary masculinities through a 'top boys' discourse that promotes competition, risk taking and the valorization of financial reward. The chapter highlights the ways in which forms of masculinity are promoted within the industry, as well as how the cultures and practices of a particular sector work to facilitate middle-class privilege. We make the case for 'top boys' as a new 21st-century form of hegemonic masculinity, where the discourse directs young men towards engaging in a symbolic struggle for masculine domination through aspiration to excel across multiple levels of success and to compete with the 'top girls' (McRobbie, 2007) who McRobbie identified as gaining a foothold on the labour market through similar but feminized processes of 'having it all'.

Chapter 7: Following Dreams and Temporary Escapes: The Impacts of Cruel Optimism

Chapter 7 focuses on 'following dreams' and considers success in the graduate labour market from graduates' perspectives of meaningful work. It does this through the lens of aspirations for jobs that are deemed to have a social worth and traces the classed and gendered experiences of two graduates. The chapter engages with the notion of 'cruel optimism' (Berlant, 2011) to explore the structural conditions of possibility that shape experiences of success. It offers two narratives as examples of contrasting classed processes of struggle and ease in labour market transitions, and as a means of demonstrating the important role of capital conversion in securing a graduate life. In doing so, we show how aspiration and capital accumulation are not enough to ensure successful labour market transitions. We argue that symbolic closure can be generated through 'cruel optimism' when aspirations are delegitimated by ideas of valued graduate activity.

Chapter 8: Lucky Breaks? Unplanned Graduate Pathways and Fateful Outcomes

Chapter 8 uses the lens of 'luck' to consider how young adults in our study understand their opportunities, obstacles, successes and failures. We analyse perceptions of luck and bad luck as explanations for apparent non-decision making or lack of strategic planning. Each of the graduates discussed in this chapter left university without a plan for what they wanted to do in terms of career. The chapter traces the ways in which their lives subsequently unfold and uses the notion of social magic to show how the embodied advantages of the privileged are misrecognized as competence and 'fit', and facilitate smoother employment transitions, even without a strategic plan.

Chapter 9: Conclusion: The Making of Graduate Lives

The final chapter of the book draws together the overall contribution of the research in a discussion focused on rethinking constructions of graduate success. In particular, the chapter draws out the significance of the material and the symbolic in graduate employment, and highlights the importance to graduates in our study of not just making a living, but making a life. The chapter brings together the theoretical tools we have used to open up a conversation about re-imagining constructions of graduate success. We end with a reflection on doing longitudinal qualitative inquiry.

References

Allen, K. (2014) 'Blair's children': young women as 'aspirational subjects' in the psychic landscape of class, *The Sociological Review*, 62(4): 760–79.

Bathmaker, A.M. (2018) Seeking distinction and addressing inequalities: an analysis of new times for college-based higher education in England, in J. Gallacher and F. Reeve (eds) *New Frontiers for College Education: International Perspectives*, London: Routledge, pp 167–81.

Bathmaker, A.M. and Bowl, M. (2018) Institutional diversification and student diversity in English higher education: in M. Bowl, C. McCaig and J. Hughes (eds) *Equality and Differentiation in Marketised Higher Education: A New Level Playing Field?*, Switzerland: Palgrave Macmillan, pp 119–48.

Bathmaker, A.M., Ingram, N. and Waller, R. (2013) Higher education, social class and the mobilisation of capitals: knowing and playing the game, *British Journal of Sociology of Education*, 34(5–6: Special Issue on Education and Social Mobility): 723–43.

Bathmaker, A.M., Ingram, N., Abrahams, J., Hoare, A., Waller, R. and Bradley, H. (2016) *Higher Education, Social Class and Social Mobility: The Degree Generation*, London: Palgrave Macmillan.

Berlant, L. (2011) *Cruel Optimism*, Durham, NC: Duke University Press.

Boero, G., Cook, D., Nathwani, T., Naylor, R. and Smith, J. (2019) The return to a degree: new evidence based on the birth cohort studies and the labour force survey, HESA, www.hesa.ac.uk/files/Return_to_a_degree_main_report.pdf

Boliver, V. (2011) Expansion, differentiation, and the persistence of social class inequalities in British higher education, *Higher Education*, 61: 229–42.

Bourdieu, P. (1977) *Outline of a Theory of Practice*, Cambridge: Cambridge University Press.

Bourdieu, P. (1986) The forms of capital, in J. Richardson (ed) *Handbook of Theory and Research for the Sociology of Education*, Westport, CT: Greenwood, pp 241–58.

Bourdieu, P. (1989) Social space and symbolic power, *Sociological Theory*, 7(1): 14–25.

Bourdieu, P. (1990) *The Logic of Practice*, Cambridge: Polity.

Bourdieu, P. (2000) *Pascalian Meditations*, Stanford, CA: Stanford University Press.

Bourdieu, P. (2002) Habitus, in J. Hillier and E. Rooksby (eds) *Habitus: A Sense of Place*, Aldershot: Ashgate, pp 27–34.

Bourdieu, P. and Eagleton, T. (1992) Doxa and common life, *New Left Review*, I(191): 111–21.

Bowl, M., McCaig, C. and Hughes, J. (eds) (2018) *Equality and Differentiation in Marketised Higher Education: A New Level Playing Field?*, Switzerland: Palgrave Macmillan.

Brooks, R. (2018a) Understanding the higher education student in Europe: a comparative analysis, *Compare: A Journal of Comparative and International Education*, 48(4): 500–17.

Brooks, R. (2018b) The construction of higher education students in English policy documents, *British Journal of Sociology of Education*, 39(6): 745–61.

Brooks, R. (2019) The construction of higher education students within national policy: a cross-European comparison, *Compare: A Journal of Comparative and International Education*, 52(2): 161–80.

Brooks, R. and Abrahams, J. (2020) European higher education students: contested constructions, *Sociological Research Online*, 25(2): 273–88.

Brown, P. (2003) The opportunity trap: education and employment in a global economy, *European Educational Research Journal*, 2(1): 141–79.

Brown, P., Lauder, H. and Ashton, D. (2011) *The Global Auction: The Broken Promises of Education, Jobs and Income*, Oxford: Oxford University Press.

Browne, J. (2010) Securing a sustainable future for higher education, Department for Business, Innovation and Skills, https://assets.publishing.service.gov.uk/government/uploads/system/uploads/attachment_data/file/422565/bis-10-1208-securing-sustainable-higher-education-browne-report.pdf

Burke, C. (2016) *Culture, Capitals and Graduate Futures: Degrees of Class*, London: Routledge and Society for Research into Higher Education.

Burke, C. and Christie, F. (2019) *Graduate Careers in Context*, Abingdon: Routledge.

Burke, C., Scurry, T. and Blenkinsopp, J. (2019) Navigating the graduate labour market: the impact of social class on student understandings of graduate careers and the labour market, *Studies in Higher Education*, 45(8): 1711–22.

Business, Innovation and Skills Committee (2016) *The Teaching Excellence Framework: Assessing Quality in Higher Education: Third Report of Session 2015–2016*, London: House of Commons Stationery Office Limited, https://publications.parliament.uk/pa/cm201516/cmselect/cmbis/572/572.pdf

Christie, F. (2019) Competing voices: a figured worlds approach to theorising graduate perspectives on career success, *International Studies in Sociology of Education*, 28(3–4): 326–44.

Cunningham, N. and Savage, M. (2015) The secret garden? Elite metropolitan geographies in the UK, *Sociological Review*, 63(2): 321–58.

DBIS (Department for Business, Innovation and Skills) (2011) *Participation Rates in Higher Education: Academic Years 2006/2007–2009/2010*, London: HMSO.

DES (Department of Education and Science) (1991) *Higher Education: A New Framework*, London: HMSO.

DfES (Department for Education and Skills) (2003) *The Future of Higher Education*, London: HMSO.

Donelan, M. (2020) Universities minister calls for true social mobility, www.gov.uk/government/speeches/universities-minister-calls-for-true-social-mobility

Elias, P., Purcell, K., Atfield, G., Kispeter, E., Day, R. and Poole, S. (2021) Ten years on – the Futuretrack graduates, Warwick Institute for Employment Research, https://warwick.ac.uk/fac/soc/ier/futu retrack/hp-contents/ten_years_on_-the_futuretrack_graduates_f ull_report_28_july_2021.pdf

Finn, K., Ingram, N. and Allen, K. (2021) Student millennials/ millennial students: how the lens of generation constructs understandings of the contemporary higher education student, in R. Brooks and S. O'Shea (eds) *Reimagining the Higher Education Student*, Abingdon: Routledge, pp 187–204.

Friedman, S., Laurison, D. and Macmillan, L. (2017) *Social Mobility, the Class Pay Gap and Intergenerational Worklessness: New Insights from the Labour Force Survey*, London: Social Mobility Commission.

Giddens, A. (1991) *Modernity and Self-Identity: Self and Society in the Late Modern Age*, Cambridge: Polity.

Glaesser, J. and Cooper, B. (2013) Using rational action theory and Bourdieu's habitus theory together to account for educational decision-making in England and Germany, *Sociology*, 48(3): 463–81.

Goldthorpe, J.H. (2007) *On Sociology, Second Edition, Volume One: Critique and Program*, Stanford, CA: Stanford University Press.

Goldthorpe, J.H. (2016) Social class mobility in modern Britain: changing structure, constant process, *Journal of the British Academy*, 4: 89–111.

HESA (Higher Education Statistics Agency) (2021) Higher education graduate outcomes statistics: UK, 2018/19 – summary, www.hesa. ac.uk/news/20-07-2021/sb260-higher-education-graduate-outco mes-statistics

Hoare, A.G. and Corver, M. (2010) The regional geography of new young graduate labour in the UK, *Regional Studies*, 44(4): 477–94.

Hodkinson, P. and Sparkes, A. (1997) Careership: a sociological theory of career decision making, *British Journal of Sociology of Education*, 18(1): 29–44.

Holland, J. and Thomson, R. (2009) Gaining perspective on choice and fate, *European Societies*, 11(3): 451–69.

Houghton, E. (2019) Impersonal statements: aspiration and cruel optimism in the English higher education application process, *International Studies in Sociology of Education*, 28(3–4): 279–98.

Ingram, N. and Allen, K. (2019) 'Talent-spotting' or 'social magic'? Inequality, cultural sorting and constructions of the ideal graduate in elite professions, *The Sociological Review*, 67(3): 723–40.

Ingram, N. and Gamsu, S. (2022) Talking the talk of social mobility: the political performance of a misguided agenda, *Sociological Research Online*, 27(1): 189–206.

McRobbie, A. (2007) 'Top girls?', *Cultural Studies*, 21(4–5): 718–37.

Mendick, H., Allen, K., Harvey, L. and Ahmad, A. (2018) *Celebrity, Aspiration, and Contemporary Youth: Education and Inequality in an Era of Austerity*, London: Bloomsbury.

Milburn, A. (2009) *Unleashing Aspirations: Final Report of the Panel on Fair Access to the Professions*, London: Cabinet Office.

Milburn, A. (2012a) *Fair Access to Professional Careers: Report by Independent Reviewer on Social Mobility and Child Poverty*, London: Cabinet Office.

Milburn, A. (2012b) *University Challenge: How Higher Education Can Advance Social Mobility*, London: Assets Publishing service, https://assets.publishing.service.gov.uk/government/uploads/system/uploads/attachment_data/file/80188/Higher-Education.pdf

Moreau, M.P. and Leathwood, C. (2006) Graduates' employment and the discourse of employability: a critical analysis, *Journal of Education and Work*, 19(4): 305–24.

Morrin, K. (2015) Unresolved reflections: Bourdieu, haunting and struggling with ghosts, in J. Thatcher, N. Ingram, C. Burke and J. Abrahams (eds) *Bourdieu: The Next Generation: The Development of Bourdieu's Intellectual Heritage in Contemporary UK Sociology*, Abingdon: Routledge, pp 123–39.

Morrison, A. (2019) Whose employability? Fees, labour markets and the unequal rewards of undergraduate study, in F. Christie and C. Burke (eds) *Graduate Careers in Context: Research, Policy and Practice*, Abingdon: Routledge, pp 29–40.

OfS (Office for Students) (2021) A geography of employment and earnings: autumn 2021, https://www.officeforstudents.org.uk/media/45bc055c-a06b-4ea6-a344-0b050cacca3a/geography-of-employment-and-earnings-autumn-2021-update.pdf

ONS (Office for National Statistics) (2013) Graduates in the UK labour market: 2013, www.ons.gov.uk/employmentandlabourmarket/peopleinwork/employmentandemployeetypes/articles/graduatesintheuklabourmarket/2013-11-19#graduates-in-the-uk-labour-market-2013

Public Accounts Committee (2009) *Widening Participation in Higher Education: Fourth Report of Session 2008–2009*, London: House of Commons Stationery Office Limited, https://publications.parliament.uk/pa/cm200809/cmselect/cmpubacc/226/9780215526557.pdf

Purcell, K., Elias, P., Atfield, G., Behle, H., Ellison, R. and Luchinskaya, D. (2013) *Transitions into Employment, Further Study and Other Outcomes: The Futuretrack Stage 4 Report*, Manchester and Coventry: HECSU and Warwick Institute for Employment Research.

Rivera, L. (2012) Diversity within reach: recruitment versus hiring in elite firms, *Annals of the American Academy of Political and Social Science*, 639: 70–89.

Rivera, L. (2015) *Pedigree: How Elite Students Get Elite Jobs*, Princeton, NJ: Princeton University Press.

Sage, J., Evandrou, M. and Falkingham, J. (2013) Onwards or homewards? Complex graduate migration pathways, wellbeing and the 'parental safety net', *Population, Space and Place*, 19(6): 738–55.

Social Mobility Commission (2019) *State of the Nation 2018–19: Social Mobility in Great Britain*, London: Social Mobility Commission, www.gov.uk/government/publications/social-mobility-in-great-britain-state-of-the-nation-2018-to-2019

Social Mobility Commission (2020) *Monitoring Social Mobility. 2013–2020: Is the Government Delivering on Our Recommendations?*, London: Social Mobility Commission, www.gov.uk/government/publications/monitoring-social-mobility-2013-to-2020

Tholen, G. (2017a) Symbolic closure: towards a renewed sociological perspective on the relationship between higher education, credentials and the graduate labour market, *Sociology*, 51(5): 1067–83.

Tholen, G. (2017b) *Graduate Work*, Oxford: Oxford University Press.

Tholen, G. and Brown, P. (2017) Higher education and the myth of graduate employability, in R. Waller, N. Ingram and M. Ward (eds) *Higher Education and Social Inequalities: University Admissions, Experiences and Outcomes*, Abingdon: Routledge, pp 153–66.

Threadgold, S. (2020) *Bourdieu and Affect: Towards a Theory of Affective Affinities*, Bristol: Bristol University Press.

Tomlinson, M. (2008) 'The degree is not enough': students' perceptions of the role of higher education credentials for graduate work and employability, *British Journal of Sociology of Education*, 29(1): 49–61.

Tomlinson, M. (2017) Forms of graduate capital and their relationship to graduate employability, *Education and Training*, 59(4): 338–52.

Wallace, D. (2019) Making moral migrants? Exploring the educational aspirations of Black African and Caribbean boys in a New York City public school, *International Studies in Sociology of Education*, 28(3–4): 237–58.

2

Moving on Up: Researching the Lives and Careers of Young Graduates

Introduction

This book is the outcome of a longitudinal qualitative study, the Paired Peers project, which followed the progress of a cohort of young people throughout their undergraduate study and beyond into the labour market and future lives. A key goal of the research was to compare the experiences of young people from working-class and middle-class backgrounds.

While there have been major quantitative studies of graduate origins and destinations (Brown, 2006; Brown and Tannock, 2009; Purcell et al, 2009, 2013; Brown et al, 2010; Elias et al, 2021), there has been less qualitative work on graduate careers, especially of a longitudinal nature. Burke's (2016) and Tholen's (2017) studies are notable exceptions, along with Lehman's (2019, 2021) work in Canada. Very little is known about the complexity of graduate labour market transitions at the end of the 2010s, beyond the data collected by the Higher Education Statistics Agency (HESA) through the former DLHE and the current Graduate Outcomes surveys, which have captured graduate destinations at six and 15 months respectively. Our study affords an opportunity to analyse processes, opportunities and strategies – and to allow individuals to reflect on what they are doing – in a way that no other data can (Corden and Millar, 2007). The existence of a well-motivated cohort of participants provided a unique opportunity to study in real depth the lives and values of a new generation of graduates, as well as their transitions to adult lives in a post-recessionary context, at a time of national and global change in the nature of jobs and occupations.

Participants in the research all studied at either UWE or the UoB in Bristol. Bristol is the largest city in the south-west of England. Located just over 100 miles west of London, Bristol's economy in the 21st century is built on the creative media, technology, electronics and aerospace industries. Like many UK cities, Bristol has two universities: UWE, a modern university and a former polytechnic, with a focus on both teaching and research; and the UoB, a traditional 'redbrick' university (that is, one of those founded in the 19th or early 20th centuries in major British cities), which is a member of the 'elite' Russell group of universities in the UK. Participants in the research presented in this book studied at one or other of these two universities.

Phase 1 (2010–13) tracked an initial cohort of 90 middle-class and working-class students from 11 academic disciplines that were taught at both universities (biological sciences, drama, economics and accountancy, engineering, English, geography, history, law, politics, psychology, and sociology). Phase 2 (2014–17) followed 56 of the original cohort over their first four years of life post-graduation. We discuss details of participant recruitment, the status and reputation of both universities, and the operationalization of social class in detail in an earlier book from Phase 1 of the project (Bathmaker et al, 2016). Here, we provide a short summary and overview to contextualize the research in the present book.

Following participants from working-class and middle-class backgrounds

In *Higher Education, Social Class and Social Mobility: The Degree Generation* (Bathmaker et al, 2016), we discuss in some detail the challenges of operationalizing a definition of class and note that how social class is conceptualized and defined is the subject of intense debates at the present time. The cultural turn in class analysis understands social class as more than about the economic and combines measures of economic, cultural and social capital to map contemporary class divisions (see, for example, Savage et al, 2013, 2015; Atkinson and Rosenlund, 2014). However, while this cultural turn in class analysis was revolutionary, a major problem facing researchers is that the forms of capital – in particular, cultural and social – are difficult to quantify and operationalize. Therefore, despite strong evidence that class is more than about the economic, official definitions in Britain today still rely on an occupational scheme, the National Statistics Socio-Economic Classification (NS-SEC), though recent research, such as that of Savage and colleagues (2013, 2015), as well as Atkinson and Rosenlund (2014), looks for new ways in which Bourdieu's theorizing can be translated into a method for classifying society. In the Paired Peers project, we used a number of indicators commonly used in the context of UK higher education to assign social class to the participants in the project.

The key variables that we used to classify students were: the occupations of parents; participation in higher education by parents; receipt of a maintenance grant or bursary; and self-assigned social class. Respondents with parents from NS-SEC Classes 1–3 were classified as middle class, while those from Classes 4–8 were classified as working class. In addition to using NS-SEC to classify parents' occupations as a key indicator of our participants' class position, we also asked for information about parents' participation in higher education. This not only provided a further basis for assigning students to a social class position, but also gave us some knowledge of the cultural resources that were available in students' families. We further asked students whether they received financial support, either from the government in the form of a maintenance grant or from their university through a bursary. Thus, we sought to develop a multifactorial approach to defining class (Bradley and Hebson, 2000). Parents' occupations and educational levels were the main indicators we used, and we turned to the other indicators where we were still doubtful. This process enabled us to recruit 90 students, 46 from UWE and 44 from UoB, at the start of the project, all of whom, based on questionnaire responses, could be securely assigned to a category of middle class or working class, as shown in Table 2.1.

At the end of Phase 1 of the project, many participants expressed an interest in continuing with their involvement if we were successful in gaining more funding. We collected contact details in

Table 2.1: Phase 1 project participants from the UoB and UWE by social class and gender

	UWE working class	UWE middle class	UoB working class	UoB middle class
Female	12	11	15	11
Male	12	11	6	12
Total	24	22	21	23

the latter interview stages of Phase 1, which was just before final exams and graduation in the spring/summer of 2013. In 2014, we contacted the participants by email and text message to request participation in Phase 2 and received 56 positive responses, a cohort we retained for a further three years until the completion of data collection in 2017 (for a demographic overview of participants, see Table 2.2). Interviews for phase 2 began in Autumn 2014, approximately one year after completion of undergraduate study, and continued until autumn 2017. It is important to note that continued participation in the project was voluntary, which led to an imbalance in our categories with more UoB graduates than UWE agreeing to continue (34 vs 22 respectively); more middle-class than working-class (33 vs 23 respectively); and more women than men (30 vs 26 respectively). We recognize that the participants who self-selected to remain in the project perhaps did so because they felt satisfied with their early labour market transitions and were comfortable talking about their lives. We cannot make assumptions about the experiences of those who did not remain involved in the project but it is interesting to note that those who did were all in employment when we first caught up with them.

We recognize that in our initial categorizations of the students, we assumed a gender binary of male and female (see Tables 2.1 and 2.2) and now acknowledge this as a limitation of our study. We outline our approach to recruitment in Bathmaker et al (2016), but it is salient to this discussion to highlight that in an initial questionnaire, we offered participants the categories of male and female against which to define themselves. We recognize now that our sampling strategy did not leave the project open to the possibility of gender

Table 2.2: Phase 2 project participants from the UoB and UWE by social class and gender

	UWE working class	UWE middle class	UoB working class	UoB middle class
Female	4	7	10	9
Male	5	6	4	11
Total	9	13	14	20

diversity (Nowakowsi et al, 2016; Lindqvist et al, 2021). In the 12 years since conducting the initial questionnaire, awareness of issues of gender diversity has increased, and while none of the participants challenged or discussed the binary (and given the strong rapport we developed with them over a seven-year period, it is likely that they would have trusted us enough to make this challenge), in hindsight, we see a missed opportunity for opening the project to generating insights around gender diversity and higher education.

In the rest of the book, we identify graduates as either male or female, and middle class or working class, based on the initial classification outlined earlier. However, we are aware that our binary classification masks fractions within classes that have been identified in most forms of class theory, including that of Bourdieu, which further differentiate the positions and orientations regarding graduate futures and employment of the young graduates in this study.

Classic Weberian analysis identifies fractions in the working class on the basis of their skill (skilled, semi-skilled and unskilled) (Bradley, 2016). In earlier work (Fielding et al, 1995), Savage and colleagues distinguished between a managerial, predominantly private sector, fraction of the middle class with high levels of economic capital, and a professional, often public sector, fraction characterized by high levels of cultural capital. Their account was influenced by the work of Bourdieu (1984 [1979]), for whom classes are divided internally according to the relative preponderance of economic or cultural capitals possessed by incumbents. Weininger (2002: 127–8) summarizes Bourdieu's understanding of class fractions as follows:

Occupational categories within the dominant class are differentiated from one another such that professors and 'artistic producers' – the occupations whose incumbents hold the greatest cultural capital and the least economic capital – are opposed to industrialists and commercial employers – the occupations whose incumbents hold a preponderance of economic capital but relatively little cultural capital. Located in between these two polar extremes are the professions, whose incumbents have roughly equal amounts of economic and social capital. In a similar manner, the petty bourgeoisie is differentiated between small business owners, endowed primarily with economic capital, and primary school teachers, endowed primarily with cultural capital. Located in an intermediate position between them are categories such as technicians, office workers, and secretaries.

In the Paired Peers study, differences among students based on this more specific account of social class background became increasingly apparent in the narratives of students while they were undergraduates. These differences continued as young people progressed from university to graduate lives. At the same time, the chapters in this book reveal how variations in the social class positioning of participants' families can be traced through into how young people were able to take advantage of the opportunities that higher education can offer and how this played out in transitions beyond higher education. We are therefore able to explore the changing nature of class reproduction and its intersections with gender, ethnicity and age. We consider what it means to have a classed identity and how this may be changed through processes of education. We also seek to explore the ways in which privilege is maintained in the shifting social field of graduate employment and illuminate the processes of habitus-to-field adjustment that advantage the middle class and the role of these factors in the maintenance of class divisions.

While the central focus of our study is social class, our analysis also explores the ways in which class intersects with race, recognizing that 'class factors articulate with "race" and ethnicity to produce complex patterns of participation in higher education' (Brah and Phoenix, 2004: 82). The complex and contradictory ways in which class works, for both middle-class and working-class Black, Asian and Minority Ethnic (BAME) populations in England, has become a focus of increasing attention in research (see, for example, Reay et al, 2005; Reay, 2008; Shah et al, 2010; Archer, 2011; Basit, 2013; Rollock et al, 2015). This work draws on theories of intersectionality, which direct attention to how axes of differentiation work together to create specific conditions of disadvantage (or advantage). Following on from Crenshaw's (1990 [1989], 1991) work in the US in the 1990s, Brah and Phoenix (2004: 75) have argued that studying the intersection of class, gender and ethnicity 'allows a more complex and dynamic understanding than a focus on social class alone'. Brah and Phoenix (2004: 76) define intersectionality as follows:

> We regard the concept of 'intersectionality' as signifying the complex, irreducible, varied, and variable effects which ensue when multiple axes of differentiation – economic, political, cultural, psychic, subjective and experiential – intersect in historically specific contexts. The concept emphasizes that different dimensions of social life cannot be separated out into discrete and pure strands.

We employ the terms 'ethnicity' and 'race' at various points in the book to cover a range of identities, and indicate each participant's ethnicity when we first introduce them. The majority of the participants in both phases of the project were white, and we have discussed the ethnic make-up of our sample at both universities in Bathmaker et al (2016). We also engage in discussions of white privilege. 'Whiteness' theory suggests that 'whiteness is largely invisible to whites' (Owen, 2007: 206); it is simply the natural order of things (Rollock, 2014), creating what Gillborn (2008: 162) has referred to as a 'whiteworld'. In Bathmaker et al (2016), we discussed the 'unspoken whiteness of the academy' and highlighted how it can go unnoticed and uncommented upon (Clegg et al, 2003: 163–4) – what Mirza (2006: 106) calls 'normative whiteness'. In the present book, we continue this analysis to consider the white spaces of the graduate labour market, drawing on Puwar's (2004) framework of space invaders, and consider how white bodies are constructed as the somatic norm.

A key strength of our project was being able to follow participants over three years of undergraduate study and four years post-graduation. At the same time, we are aware that volunteering to participate in a longitudinal study requires enthusiasm and willingness to engage with a research project, and the sample that we followed consisted of participants who were prepared to spend time reflecting on their experience and continuing to talk to us about it as they sought to establish their lives and careers after university.

Data collection and analysis

The main method of data collection involved in-depth biographical interviews of one to one-and-a-half hours, using a semi-structured interview schedule. Following on from six interviews during Phase 1 of the project, participants were interviewed four times in Phase 2: the first (Interview 7) at the commencement of Phase 2 of the project; and the second (Interview 8) to assess progress one year on. Two further interviews (Interviews 9 and 10), one per year, tracked subsequent developments. The interviews covered a wide range of topics related to making a life and career post-university, including career planning, employment and unemployment, further study, experience of work, further acquisition and mobilization of capitals (especially social contacts), contact with family, significant relationships, accommodation and living arrangements, leisure activities, travel, transport and mobility, debts and finances, and health and well-being.

While interviews were conducted face to face in Phase 1, during Phase 2 (the graduate phase of the project), they were conducted either face to face or via Skype, as participants were spread geographically across the UK and other parts of the world. We maintained links with participants during the course of these four years via email and a Facebook page in order to sustain continuity of communication and minimize attrition. We offered each participant two interviews in the first year and then one annual interview in the two successive years. Fitting in with participants' busy lives was complex, and in some cases, we combined two interviews into one interview encounter in order to accommodate the scheduling difficulties we experienced. Where possible, we conducted Interview 7 (the first interview in Phase 2) in person. For Interviews 8 to 10, we used a combination of face-to-face and online interviews. We aimed for Interview 7 to be in person because we wanted to establish and/or re-establish rapport between interviewee and interviewer. In our first book, we write about the importance of this dynamic in maintaining the enthusiasm of the cohort for the duration of the data collection (Bathmaker et al, 2016). Two of the interviewers (Abrahams and Ingram) had conducted most of the interviews in Phase 1 of the project and continued with a select sample each in Phase 2. Another four of the interviewers (Bathmaker, Bradley, Hoare and Waller) were investigators in Phase 1 of the project and had met the participants at annual dissemination events. Three of the interviewers (Bentley, Papafilippou and Ward) were new to the project. Ward left the project after the first round of interviews, and Bentley and Papafilippou worked full-time on the project and conducted the majority of the interviews over its duration. In total, Phase 1 of the project generated approximately 570 hours of interview data, while Phase 2 generated approximately 300 hours. This book, therefore, offers an analysis of a substantial and unique qualitative data set of over 800 hours of interview material collected over a seven-year period, documenting the lives of young people throughout their time at university and into the first four years of graduate life.

All interviews were recorded and transcribed. We undertook preliminary analysis of the data using NVivo software, following a content analysis approach and using thematic codes that were agreed through discussion in the research team. These codes were identified from a combination of our reading the data, our reading of existing research literature and the use of a conceptual frame that drew on the work of Bourdieu, which made us alert to issues of habitus, capitals and social fields, and especially to the capital conversion process.

The wider context of the data

In 2013, the participants in the Paired Peers project graduated from three-year undergraduate study. The national picture for

UK-domiciled leavers among this cohort six months after graduation shows that 60 per cent were in full-time employment, 12.3 per cent were in further study and 5 per cent were unemployed (DLHE survey 2014/15, HESA). From this wider data set, we matched, at an individual student level, the UoB and UWE undergraduate records of the two 2010-entry Paired Peers cohorts with their subsequent DLHE returns, some six months after graduation. It is important to note that the DLHE has been criticized for garnering short-term graduate snapshots, rather than providing a longer-term picture of graduate destinations, which led to it being replaced by a survey that captures outcomes at 18 months post-graduation. However, for our cohort, it is the only suitable source available, and it provides an interesting broader overview.

The data show that a similar percentage of graduates from both universities were in full-time employment six months after graduation (58 per cent of UWE graduates and 56 per cent of UoB graduates), in line with the national picture of destinations (60 per cent in full-time employment). However, there are differences on closer inspection. The data on employment show that UWE graduates outperform UoB graduates in terms of moving into work within six months of graduation. UWE's combined percentage of graduates in full- and part-time employment is over 10 percentage points higher than that of the UoB (77 per cent compared to 65 per cent). Moreover, while both universities had an above-national-average (12.3 per cent) percentage of graduates in full-time education, the UoB scored higher on this measure than UWE (20 per cent and 13.3 per cent, respectively). With regard to unemployment, only 1.3 per cent of UWE graduates reported being unemployed, compared to 5.2 per cent of UoB graduates, the latter close to the national average of 5 per cent. In simple terms, UoB graduates were more likely to be in full-time study, whereas UWE graduates were less likely to be unemployed. However, when income is taken into account, the picture looks quite different.

The odds of a UoB graduate in full-time work earning £25,000 or more annually were much higher than they were for their UWE equivalents (14.5 times greater), though UoB graduates also had four times the odds of being unemployed. UoB graduates were very much more likely not only to be earning higher salaries, but also to be in a 'graduate'-rated job and, closely linked, to consider their first degree as a formal requirement for employment, though not through its specific subject matter. DLHE respondents from UWE in full-time employment were more likely to rate their first-degree *subject*, rather than its *level*, as important in securing work and to draw on personal contacts (friends and family) as their initial information source.

While this provides an interesting overview of destinations six months after graduation, the statistics raise questions about what is happening in the transition to the graduate labour market that facilitates these patterns. Why are UWE students going straight into work while a higher percentage of their UoB counterparts remain unemployed after six months? Why are UoB graduates more likely to be earning higher salaries and doing 'graduate work' than the UWE cohort? Our rich data set sheds light on the processes that generate these outcomes by providing an in-depth look at the experiences of a range of graduates and following them over a much more prolonged period (for an overview of the final interview employment destinations of each participant, see Appendix). In what follows, we have selected narratives that reflect these trends, as well as counter-narratives that capture the diversity of experiences in terms of class, gender and, where possible, race. In doing so, we provide unique insight into the processes of making a graduate life.

References

Archer, L. (2011) Constructing minority ethnic middle-class identity: an exploratory study with parents, pupils and young professionals, *Sociology*, 45(1): 134–51.

Atkinson, W. and Rosenlund, L. (2014) Mapping the British social space: toward a Bourdieusian class scheme, SPAIS Working Paper 02–14, University of Bristol, www.bristol.ac.uk/spais/research/workingpapers/

Basit, T.N. (2013) Educational capital as a catalyst for upward social mobility amongst British Asians: a three-generational analysis, *British Educational Research Journal*, 39(4): 714–32.

Bathmaker, A.M., Ingram, I., Abrahams, J., Hoare, T., Waller, R. and Bradley, H. (2016) *Higher Education, Social Class and Social Mobility: The Degree Generation*, London: Palgrave Macmillan.

Bourdieu, P. (1984 [1979]) *Distinction: A Social Critique of the Judgement of Taste* (trans R. Nice), London: Routledge.

Bradley, H. (2016) *Fractured Identities* (2nd edn), Cambridge: Polity.

Bradley, H. and Hebson, G. (2000) Breaking the silence: the need to re-articulate class, *International Journal of Sociology and Social Policy*, 19(9/10/11): 187–209.

Brah, A. and Phoenix, A. (2004) Ain't I a woman? Revisiting intersectionality, *Journal of International Women's Studies*, 5(3): 75–86.

Brown, P. (2006) The opportunity trap, in H. Lauder, P. Brown, J.A. Dillabough and A.H. Halsey (eds) *Education, Globalization and Social Change*, Oxford: Oxford University Press, pp 381–97.

Brown, P. and Tannock, S. (2009) Education, meritocracy and the global war for talent, *Journal of Education Policy*, 24(4): 377–92.

Brown, P., Lauder, H. and Ashton, D. (2010) *The Global Auction: The Broken Promises of Education, Jobs and Incomes*, Oxford: Oxford University Press.

Burke, C. (2016) *Culture, Capitals and Graduate Futures: Degrees of Class*, London: Routledge.

Clegg, S., Parr, S. and Wan, S. (2003) Racialising discourses in higher education, *Teaching in Higher Education*, 8(2): 155–68.

Corden, A. and Millar, J. (2007) Time and change: a review of the qualitative longitudinal research literature for social policy, *Social Policy and Society*, 6(4): 583.

Crenshaw, K. (1990 [1989]) Demarginalizing the intersection of race and sex: a black feminist critique of antidiscrimination doctrine, feminist theory and antiracist politics, University of Chicago Legal Forum, 139–67, in D. Kairys (ed) *The Politics of Law: A Progressive Critique*, New York: Pantheon, pp 195–217.

Crenshaw, K. (1991) Mapping the margins: intersectionality, identity politics, and violence against women of color, *Stanford Law Review*, 43(6): 1241–99.

Elias, P., Purcell, K., Atfield, G., Kispeter, E., Day, R. and Poole, S. (2021) Ten years on – the Futuretrack graduates, Warwick Institute for Employment Research, https://warwick.ac.uk/fac/soc/ier/futu retrack/hp-contents/ten_years_on_-the_futuretrack_graduates_f ull_report_28_july_2021.pdf

Fielding, T., Savage, M., Dickens, P. and Barlow, J. (1995) *Property, Bureaucracy and Culture: Middle-Class Formation in Contemporary Britain*, London: Routledge.

Gillborn, D. (2008) *Racism and Education: Coincidence or Conspiracy?*, Abingdon: Routledge.

Ingram, N. and Allen, K. (2019) 'Talent-spotting' or 'social magic'? Inequality, cultural sorting and constructions of the ideal graduate in elite professions, *The Sociological Review*, 67(3): 723–40.

Lehmann, W. (2019) Forms of capital in working-class students' transition from university to employment, *Journal of Education and Work*, 32(4): 347–59.

Lehmann, W. (2021) Conflict and contentment: case study of the social mobility of working-class students in Canada, *European Journal of Education*, 56(1): 41–52.

Lindqvist, A., Gustafsson Sendén, M. and Renström, E.A. (2021) What is gender, anyway: a review of the options for operationalising gender, *Psychology & Sexuality*, 12(4): 332–44.

Mirza, H.S. (2006) Transcendence over diversity: black women in the academy, *Policy Futures in Education*, 4(2): 101–13.

Nowakowski, A.C., Sumerau, J. and Mathers, L.A. (2016) None of the above: strategies for inclusive teaching with 'representative' data, *Teaching Sociology*, 44(2): 96–105.

Owen, D.S. (2007) Towards a critical theory of whiteness, *Philosophy & Social Criticism*, 33(2): 203–22.

Purcell, K., Elias, P., Atfield, G., Behle, H. and Ellison, R. (2009) Plans, aspirations and realities: taking stock of higher education and career choices one year on: findings from the second Futuretrack survey of 2006 applicants for UK Higher education, November, https://warwick.ac.uk/fac/soc/ier/futuretrack/findings/futuretrack_stage_2_report_plans_aspirations_and_realities.pdf

Purcell, K., Elias, P., Atfield, G., Behle, H., Ellison, R. and Luchinskaya, D. (2013) *Transitions into Employment, Further Study and Other Outcomes: The Futuretrack Stage 4 Report*, Manchester and Coventry: HECSU and Warwick Institute for Employment Research.

Puwar, N. (2004) *Space Invaders: Race, Gender and Bodies Out of Place*, Oxford: Berg.

Reay, D. (2008) Class out of place: the white middle classes and intersectionalities of class and 'race' in urban state schooling in England, in L. Weis (ed) *The Way Class Works*, New York: Routledge, pp 87–99.

Reay, D., David, M.E. and Ball, S. (2005) *Degrees of Choice: Social Class, Race and Gender in Higher Education*, Stoke-on-Trent: Trentham Books.

Rollock, N. (2014) Race, class and 'the harmony of dispositions', *Sociology*, 48(3): 445–51.

Rollock, N., Gillborn, D., Vincent, C. and Ball, S. (2015) *The Colour of Class: The Educational Strategies of the Black Middle Classes*, Abingdon and New York: Routledge.

Savage, M., Devine, F., Cunningham, N., Taylor, M., Li, Y., Hjellbrekke, J., Le Roux, B. et al (2013) A new model of social class? Findings from the BBC's Great British Class Survey experiment, *Sociology*, 47(2): 219–50.

Savage, M., Cunningham, N., Devine, F., Friedman, S., Laurison, D., McKenzie, L. et al (2015) *Social Class in the 21st Century*, London: Penguin.

Shah, B., Dwyer, C. and Modood, T. (2010) Explaining educational achievement and career aspirations among young British Pakistanis: mobilizing 'ethnic capital'? *Sociology*, 44(6): 1109–27.

Tholen, G. (2017) *Graduate Work*, Oxford: Oxford University Press.

Weininger, E.B. (2002) Pierre Bourdieu on social class and symbolic violence, in E.O. Wright (ed) *Alternative Foundations of Class Analysis*, pp 119–71.

3

London Calling: Being Mobile and Mobilizing Capitals

Introduction

This chapter takes as its focus access to graduate employment opportunities in London and considers the role of the capital city in the reproduction of inequality. While graduate employment in professional and management positions is available across the UK, the Social Mobility Commission (2019) documents how London has seen a disproportionate growth in these positions in comparison to the rest of the UK, with 45 per cent of new jobs at this level being created in the capital. London is also widely recognized as a hub for elite graduate recruiters, particularly in respect to jobs in finance, law and IT.

The recruitment practices of these and other industries located in London have regularly been found to favour those who are already advantaged, effectively reproducing class inequalities. Cook et al (2012), for example, found that privately educated graduates were 13 times more likely to be employed in a London law firm than their state-educated peers. Through analysis of the recruitment and selection procedures of these firms, they conclude that these practices reproduce inequalities because they rely heavily on forms of symbolic capital to which the privileged have greater access. They discuss a specific 'City effect', where the culture of law firms conforms to the doxa of the field in recruiting the elite, something very much replicated in other elite industries in the city. Oakley et al (2017) draw similar conclusions in relation to the cultural and creative industries. Through analysis of the national Labour Force Survey, they highlight how the privileged dominate the sector, especially in London, with over 60 per cent of those employed in the cultural and creative industries in London coming from professional/managerial backgrounds, while the figure for the rest of the UK is roughly 45 per cent.

This pattern of recruitment practices then extends into a distinctive class pay gap within managerial and professional positions. Findings from the Social Mobility Commission's (2019) 'State of the nation' report document that those in professional or managerial occupations from working-class backgrounds earn 17 per cent per year less than their colleagues from more privileged backgrounds, and Friedman, Laurison and Macmillan (2017) note an average pay gap of £10,660 per year for those from working-class backgrounds compared to those from professional or managerial backgrounds. Within the cultural and creative industries specifically, Oakley et al (2017: 1526) found that the class pay gap is wider in London than elsewhere in the UK, with those from working-class backgrounds in London earning only 85 per cent of what their colleagues from professional/managerial backgrounds earn, while the figure for elsewhere in the UK is 90 per cent.

Therefore, while London has previously been described as a 'hotspot' for social mobility (Social Mobility Commission, 2016) and an 'escalator region' where meritocracy prevails, with the 'talented' and 'hard-working' able to rise to the top (Fielding, 1992), this narrative has subsequently been critiqued. A more recent report from the Social Mobility Commission (2019) demonstrates inequalities in geographical flows to London by individuals from different backgrounds. Findings indicate that those from middle-class backgrounds are three times more likely to move to London (Social Mobility Commission, 2019: 5), which has clear implications for social mobility and social justice. It could be argued that London, with its increasing domination of the share of professional/ managerial jobs, elitist recruitment and selection strategies, and significant class pay gap, rather than acting as a vehicle for social mobility, is further entrenching inequalities within labour markets.

Cunningham and Savage (2015: 338) argue that London is, in fact, an 'elite metropolitan vortex', which operates in a unique way from any other city in the UK and serves to reproduce a distinctive metropolitan elite, writing: the 'London metropolitan area is itself a vortex in which a distinctive elite formation is generated. The spatial proximity of relatively large numbers of Elite individuals is implicated in the development of distinctive cultural and social, as well as economic patterns which appear distinctive to the metropolitan Elite.' It is a city that requires – and arguably engenders the development of – elite forms of cultural, economic and social capital (Cook et al, 2012; Cunningham and Savage, 2015; Oakley et al, 2017). The proposal that London generates a 'distinctive elite formation' suggests that it is not just geographical access to London that may help or hinder graduates in gaining professional employment in the city, but a capacity to 'fit in' to the distinctive elite metropolitan milieu of the city. This is made possible through what we might tentatively call a 'London habitus', generated out of an amalgam of economic and cultural capital with geographical capital, which involves not only geographical access to London and its opportunities, but also an associated cosmopolitanism (Igarashi and Saito, 2014) that aligns with the selection criteria of elite graduate employers, who may express a desire for applicants to express global acumen (Ingram and Allen, 2019). While individuals may be encouraged to acquire and develop these attributes and capitals, for example, through university employability initiatives, for those from more privileged backgrounds, these resources and practices are anchored in the body, that is, in a habitus that involves a taken-for-granted sense of 'fit' with the metropolitan elite, built on a socially ingrained confidence and sense of entitlement. This is the social magic, or social alchemy, that Bourdieu (1990: 129) describes: 'The transformation of any kind of capital into symbolic capital, a legitimate possession grounded in the nature of its possessor, is the fundamental operation of social alchemy.' All of this renders London an important locale to look at when considering the career trajectories and geographical mobilities of the Paired Peers cohort, who entered the labour market from different social class backgrounds, having graduated from different institutions. Who can access careers in London? Who can capitalize on mobility in and out of London? If a disproportionate number of professional/managerial jobs are being created in London, it is important to consider who is able to take advantage of these opportunities. And how does the push and pull of the graduate labour market in London impact upon graduates' searches for a fulfilling and/or well-paid job? This chapter explores these questions in two ways. Initially, it utilizes the UK's DLHE dataset to present a broad mapping of which young adults are more likely to come from London prior to university alongside who ends up in London upon graduation. Subsequently, the chapter draws on qualitative data focusing primarily on the narratives of two pairs of graduates from the UoB, all white but from different social class backgrounds and genders: Nathan (male, middle class, law [also discussed in Chapter 6]), Zoe (female, working class, law), Luke (male, middle class, biology) and Freya (female, lower-middle class, biology). Nathan and Luke are both white men who are classified as coming from solidly middle-class backgrounds; Zoe and Freya are also white but are women from less advantaged backgrounds. For all four of these graduates, London features as an important part of their narratives through their capacity or incapacity to access the city and the opportunities it affords.

Through focusing on pairs of graduates from the 'elite' UoB only, the chapter considers the possibility that the 'Bristol Brand' associated with the UoB may open the door to the elite professions in London regardless of social class background. Or, is access to these professions mediated by race, class, gender and proximity to London? The chapter explores the micro-processes that render graduates more or less able to embody and capitalize upon the 'Bristol Brand'. This is examined through a Bourdieusian lens and considers how middle-class privilege facilitates access to elite professions in the capital, which is enhanced by (though not dependent upon) geographical proximity to London, as a result of which London operates as an exclusive field that further sustains and reproduces inequalities.

Who is London calling? Evidence from the DLHE

We now turn to the question of who can 'make it' to London and take up the vast career opportunities it boasts. We use data from the UK's DLHE survey,[1] looking specifically at the cohort of all

---

[1]   The DLHE survey was a statistical survey that aimed to contact UK- and European Union (EU)-domiciled graduates from higher education programmes six months after qualifying from their courses. Its aim was to establish both what type of employment

Table 3.1: Percentage of all graduates with or without London homes pre-university who are working/not working in London according to university attended

HEI	% of all graduates from London homes	% of all graduates who work in London	% of those with London homes who had a London workplace	% of those without a London home who had a London workplace
UoB	12.9	38.4	68.3	34.0
UWE	4.2	14.1	63.6	11.9

Note: 'Home' refers to the pre-university home, usually the parental home.

young people from different social class backgrounds who graduated from the two universities in Bristol, UoB and UWE, either in the same year as the Paired Peers cohort (in 2013) or in the previous or following year (in 2012 or 2014). We isolate London as a locale in the DLHE data to consider geographical flows to the capital and the interrelation of these patterns with school attended, university attended and social class background. We look at these different factors to understand how they may combine to facilitate access to labour market opportunities in London.

Table 3.1 presents the proportion of graduates who had homes in London prior to attending university (normally the parental home), as well as the proportion of graduates who took up work in London following graduation. These data are broken down according to the institution from which they graduated (UWE or UoB).

In relation to the focus of this chapter, a London home may be an important resource for those seeking employment in the capital. Table 3.1 shows that graduates from the UoB are more likely than graduates from UWE to have a pre-university London

or further study they were engaged in and their income on one specific day in the survey period. The survey was replaced in 2018 by the Graduate Outcomes survey undertaken by the HESA.

home (12.9 and 4.2 per cent, respectively), and graduates from the UoB are more likely than graduates from UWE to be working in London six months post-graduation (38.4 compared to 14.1 per cent, respectively). At the same time, the advantage of a pre-university home in London is apparent for graduates from both universities: over 60 per cent of graduates from both UWE and the UoB who had a pre-university home in London were subsequently working in London. However, there is a considerable difference between the two universities in those without a London home who moved to London for work: 34 per cent from the UoB, compared to 11.9 per cent from UWE. This suggests that the 'elite' institution may play a key role in funnelling graduates to the capital even if they do not have the advantage of a London home. This is perhaps not surprising given that elite graduate firms, largely based in London, tend to target recruitment towards students graduating from particular institutions, especially those from Russell Group universities (Ingram and Allen, 2019).

Table 3.2 looks at school attended by graduates from the two universities: independent private schools or state schools. The table shows that those who do not have a London home who attended independent schools are more likely than their state-school counterparts to move to London for work, regardless of university attended. However, privately educated UoB graduates are more likely than privately educated UWE graduates to work in London. This suggests that the capital accrued from private schooling combines with the capital gained from a Russell Group university to enhance chances on the London graduate labour market.

Table 3.3 shows a breakdown by social class background (middle class or working class) of the proportion of graduates from UWE and UoB who had homes in London prior to attending university (normally the parental home), as well as the proportion of graduates who took up work in London following graduation. As noted previously, graduates from UWE were less likely to report having a pre-university London home compared to their UoB counterparts. In Table 3.3, we can see that this applied to graduates from both working-class and middle-class backgrounds. Having a (parental) home in London can be a huge facilitator and enabler for young people when they seek graduate employment given the propensity of London-focused graduate jobs, as discussed earlier.

Table 3.2: Percentage of all graduates with or without London homes pre-university who are working/not working in London according to school attended

	HEI	% of all graduates from London homes	% of all graduates who work in London	% of those with London homes who had a London workplace	% of those without a London home who had a London workplace
State school	UoB	5.2	27.6	70	25.3
	UWE	3.5	10.3	40.0	9.3
Independent school	UoB	25.8	56.9	68.1	53.1
	UWE	7.3	34.1	*66.7*	31.6
All graduates	UoB	12.9	38.4	68.3	34.0
	UWE	4.2	14.1	63.6	11.9

Note: Cells based on less than ten total graduates are shown in italics. 'Home' refers to the pre-university home, usually the parental home.

Table 3.3 indicates that a home in London clearly acts as an enabler for graduates from not only middle-class backgrounds, but also working-class backgrounds, who are marginally more likely than those from middle-class backgrounds to have a London workplace *if* they have a pre-university London home.

Overall, though, both middle-class and working-class UoB graduates are more likely to be working in London than their respective middle-class and working-class counterparts at UWE. There also appears to be a university effect on who moves to London for work when they do not have a London home, with 25.7 per cent of UoB working-class and 35.3 per cent of UoB middle-class graduates employed in London, compared to 9.2 per cent of UWE working-class and 12.4 per cent of UWE middle-class graduates. In this case, the contrast between the two universities is more stark than making the same comparison by school type shown in Table 3.2, which indicates the potential ameliorating effects of attending private schools and/or an elite

Table 3.3: Percentage of all graduates with or without London homes pre-university who are working/not working in London according to university and social class

	HEI	% of those with London homes	% of all graduates who work in London	% of those with London homes who also had a London workplace	% of those without a London home who had a London workplace
Working class (NS-SEC 4–7)	UoB	12.8	32.0	75.0	25.7
	UWE	2.2	10.8	*83.3*	9.2
Middle class (NS-SEC 1–3)	UoB	13.0	39.3	66.7	35.3
	UWE	3.7	13.8	51.9	12.4
All graduates	UoB	12.9	38.4	68.3	34.0
	UWE	4.2	14.1	63.6	11.9

Note: Cells based on less than ten total graduates are shown in italics. 'Home' refers to the pre-university home, usually the parental home. For an explanation of social class categorization and NS-SEC, see Chapter 2.

university. The intersections with social class suggest that the status of the UoB, then, may be a crucial resource in terms of the development of social and cultural capital to facilitate transitions to the 'elite' employment field of London for students from working-class backgrounds.

Having provided an overview of key patterns showing who gains employment in London post-graduation from the two universities, we now focus at a more detailed level on the experience of participants in the Paired Peers project. Of the 56 graduates who participated in Phase 2 of the project, over one third (19) were living and/or working in London at some point during the four-year period post-graduation, as shown in Table 3.4. The split across the two institutions was relatively even, with ten graduates from the UoB living/working in London and nine UWE graduates doing so. A total of 13 of the young people were from the middle class, while

Table 3.4: Graduate participants in Phase 2 of Paired Peers living/
working in London by institution and social class background

	Total number of graduates living/ working in London	Total number of graduates working in London with pre-university London home	Working-class graduates living/ working in London	Middle-class graduates living/ working in London
UoB	10	5	4	6
UWE	9	0	2	7
Total	19	5	6	13

only six were from working-class backgrounds. Of the six who were from working-class backgrounds, four had graduated from the UoB compared to two from UWE. Only five of the graduates working in London also had pre-university homes in London, all of them from the UoB.

In what follows, we present the narratives of four participants, all of whom sought to work in London. These four narratives have been selected because they provide insights into the ways in which individuals seek to mobilize and convert capitals that are valued on the labour market in London to enable them to succeed. First, we consider themes of privilege and proximity through the narratives of Freya and Luke, both of whom were able to combine the advantages of a family home in London with a socially ingrained confidence and sense of entitlement that enabled them to successfully 'fit' into the cultures and practices of London labour markets. Following this, we consider the experiences of Nathan and Zoe, and explore what factors enable or constrain the possibility of making the move into London for graduate work.

Privilege and proximity: belonging to the elite metropolitan vortex

Freya and Luke, both biology graduates, had family homes in London, and both returned 'home' on graduation. Four years later, they had each generated enough capital to move out of the family home, and in their final interviews, both were cohabiting with a partner in London. In what follows, we discuss Freya's and Luke's career aspirations and steps taken in pursuit of achieving their goals, arguing that their narratives demonstrate the working of a 'London habitus'. While they both had ready access to London, which afforded them a particular form of privilege, they were able to combine this with economic and cultural capitals, as well as dispositions, which enabled them to actively construct successful careers in a context where cosmopolitanism and global acumen are prized.

Freya is a white woman from a lower-middle-class background, whose parents' class positions were classified as NS-SEC 3 and 5. Neither of her parents had higher education qualifications, and in Bourdieusian terms, we might understand Freya's family class position in terms of having more economic than symbolically recognized cultural capital, positioning her at the borderline of middle and working class. For Freya, having a London home facilitated her potential to combine the cultural capital gained from her degree qualification with the economic security she needed to creatively explore post-university opportunities. As she explained:

> 'Now I'm home, no one's pressuring me to do it [work]. I think my parents are just, like, "Do whatever you need to do", kind of thing. They tried to offer to pay off my overdraft and I was, like, "No, I want to do it myself." But, like, obviously, I don't pay rent in my parents' house, or food or anything, but I really want to actually, like, have money saved up. I do want to move out, but that's not, like, any plausible thing on the horizon right now.'

Returning to a family home to live without financial obligations is a luxury not afforded to all and provides a clear economic advantage (see Chapter 8) regardless of the locale. The advantage is more acute in the context of London. Freya, then, experiencing limited financial pressure yet living in London, was afforded the luxury of time to navigate and craft a path for herself through being able to take up unpaid and low-paid opportunities on offer in the capital.

In terms of career aspiration, Freya was motivated by a passion to work with wildlife from the outset of her studies. She came to university having completed a 'gap year' in Africa, where she developed significant experience working with wild animals. Throughout her time at university, Freya maintained her commitment to this aspiration, and in the four years following graduation, she was unwavering in her pursuit of this pathway. It was here that Freya's narrative demonstrated how she was able to combine the economic resource of being able to live at home with a sense of fit and secure confidence in her capacities, which enabled her to construct a successful career pathway for herself.

Initially, Freya secured an unpaid internship at a major London-based institute specializing in wildlife conservation science. She then managed to capitalize upon this experience, using the internship as a foot in the door to secure herself a paid position in the organization as an administrator. The position was low paid, but since she was still living in the family home, she was able to accept work that only provided her with the financial means to get by. Alongside her admin role, Freya was given a project to work on for one day a week, which utilized her graduate skills. She also undertook a part-time postgraduate course, and four years later, she had managed to turn her admin role into a full-time permanent position working on projects that drew on her knowledge and skills in biology. Freya talked about "convincing" her manager to find money to create this (new) permanent post tailored specifically for her. Freya told us that this was made possible through working her way into the company through the unpaid internship and subsequently "proving herself". She was able to draw on the cultural capital of her degree qualification and wider experiences of working with animals to position herself as a person of value to the organization and to convince management of the need for her and her role. Her narrative shows not only how a family home in London operated as an essential resource, but also that this resource was mobilized effectively through combination with a range of other valuable capitals available to Freya, along with a habitus that harmonized with the expectations of the field, allowing her to create a graduate career for herself in the capital city.

Like Freya, Luke returned to his family home in London on graduation. Luke also had a passion for biology and wildlife.

However, unlike Freya, he recognized the lack of economic reward from a career in biology from the start of his studies and highlighted the tussle between wanting personal fulfilment and wanting to simply make money, joking that once he made his fortune, he would go and "save some pandas". Luke's aspirations wavered through his university years, and he graduated with an uncertainty over his career path yet remained solidly motivated by an aspiration for financial success. As such, returning to the family home in London, the financial capital, was the obvious next step. As Luke, like many other graduates, told us: "I wouldn't have been able to get a job doing what I'm doing anywhere else." For Luke, London was the main location offering opportunities for developing a career with a high salary. Luke was both a 'fish in water', in Bourdieusian terms (Bourdieu and Wacquant, 1992), and a strategic player in the context of the elite metropolitan vortex of London, and his privilege facilitated his capacity to land well-paid jobs in the 'congested' graduate labour market (Brown, 2013). As he told us in his first interview post-graduation: "I turned up just for the practice, really, of interviews. Got offers. … I was sitting on about six or seven offers by the time I actually accepted this one." His experience appears far removed from the stories of many other graduates battling against endless reams of job rejections. When probed, Luke talked about not actively seeking jobs, but it was apparent that he knew what was needed on a CV in order to position himself advantageously. As he explained:

> 'I've just, like, sort of meandered through life and fallen into something that's quite, like … quite lucky, which is quite good. … Well, the reason I get recruited is because of my CV. Like my grades that I've got, they're always "Might as well get him in and see what's what." It's got, like, the perfect balance of extra-curricular and academics; like, it's a CV that's going to get an interview. And once you get an interview, it's all in your hands really. If you screw up an interview, it's your own fault.'

Luke's narrative of the ease with which he could negotiate his transition to employment points to how he embodied a habitus of elite metropolitan privilege, grounded in his position in society as a white, middle-class man, the symbolic recognition of his embodied capital and the opportunities offered to mobilize his capitals to secure advantage (see also Liam's narrative in Chapter 8, whose experience of ease parallels Luke's). The geographical advantage of a family home in London was an additional key facilitator for Luke in entering the finance sector. However, it was not just access to London that facilitated this transition. Luke commented that his CV was "the perfect balance of extra-curricular and academics", arguably signalling that he was able to combine his cultural capital and 'fit' with a capacity to play the game (Bathmaker et al, 2013). Luke told us in some detail about the insidious, exclusionary recruitment strategies at play in the industry, which worked in favour of people like himself (a white, middle-class, male, heterosexual, able-bodied graduate from the UoB with top grades). Through his experience of working in recruitment consultancy, he had learned tricks to ensure his CV would 'stand out' to recruitment firms, not necessarily through outstanding contribution, but through the use of 'white text' pages:

Luke:	It's basically, you have another page in your CV that's just full of non-text that is white, so no one sees it, and if they print it off, there's nothing. But in a search engine, it will search there.
Interviewer:	So, what type of key words did you write into your CV blank page?
Luke:	Erm ... well, it was just a lot of, say, like ... I can't remember exactly, but it was all the key words, so sort of ... anything technical, like, language-wise, that they'd search, like 'graduate', erm ... 'biology', 'Bristol'. I did 'Bristol' on, like, loads of pages. I knew they were looking for that, 'Bristol University'. 'A★' as well, that was, like, just a big ream of that.

Luke told us that firms were getting wise to these tricks, but he also said that "they don't care because they're, like, 'Fair play, the guy knows his stuff'". Applicants using white text itself signalled to the recruiter that the candidate was of 'high quality' in their understanding of how to manipulate systems to work for them. In this sense, the signalling of one's privilege is disguised as disconnected from itself: it becomes 'mis'-recognized as an identifier of a highly skilled candidate.

He went on to describe his experience of being recruited for his current post in the financial industry:

> 'But anyway, this guy [recruitment agency] called me up and was just, like, "Oh yeah, I've got a job at an investment management firm doing IT", and I was, like, "How have you actually managed to find me?" And it was because of the key-word searches on my CV dealing with technology. So, I think he actually also kind of lied on my cover sheet a little bit and said that I had like practical experience with working with the technologies that I said on my CV. And I know they would have recruited me, but I've only got like theoretical knowledge. And I said this straight up in the interview because, again, I went to the interview, like, straight up, "I know nothing about the practical experience of computers", and they were, like, "That's fine, yeah". But the thing about this company is they hire … they don't hire, sort of, anyone who's proficient in IT; they hire graduates who have, like, intelligent, sort of, personas and grades. So, it's people from Oxford … or Russell.'

This extract illustrates clearly the mechanisms of inclusion in, and therefore effective exclusion from, elite firms in London through the workings of recruitment practices. We see symbolic recognition and value being attached to elite universities, including those in the Russell Group, with practical experience being negated in favour of graduates who have "intelligent … personas and grades". This poses a stark contrast to the experience of other, less privileged participants in our study, such as Adele, who attended UWE and was from a mixed-race, working-class background, and whose experience is discussed in Chapter 8. Without the symbolic legitimation afforded to white, middle-class, male graduates from the UoB, Adele continually told us of her active efforts to develop the technical experience and the social connections to try and open doors to her. Luke's taken-for-granted understanding of the recruitment practices of London companies and sense of 'fit' with their cultures meant that he could readily capitalize on the 'Bristol Brand', something that becomes misrecognized, as if by social magic, as a signifier of talent (Ingram and Allen, 2019). A process of social magic enables graduates like Luke to bypass the need for 'experience' and competence, exchanging and putting 'entitlement' in its place. Luke's understanding of the rules of the game enabled him to assert that the practical experience required by elite employers is negligible in comparison to the 'symbolic value' of his A★s at A-Level and UoB bachelor's degree. He confidently worked the system and replaced the specific experience necessary with more generalized cultural capital acquired through a degree from a Russell Group university, augmented and legitimated by embodied privilege. In Luke's case, the enabling capital of a Russell Group degree intersects with privilege and geographical proximity to London, which together facilitate and support this phenomenon of social magic.

Fitting and not fitting in: the making and not making of a life and career in London

In contrast to Freya and Luke, neither Nathan nor Zoe had a family home in London. However, in line with patterns noted in the DLHE data outlined earlier, this proved to be more prohibitive for Zoe (a white, working-class female) than for Nathan (a white, middle-class male). Both graduates aspired to careers in professional industries (law and finance, respectively), where opportunities for high remuneration were concentrated around London. Four years after graduation, Nathan was living and working in London, but Zoe remained in her home place. In what follows, we discuss Nathan's and Zoe's career aspirations, and explore the steps taken in pursuit of these. Here, we argue that living and working in London requires a 'London habitus', that is, a privileged habitus that operates through possession of economic and social capital that affords, and is furthered by, the capacity to take risks to successfully move to London for life and work.

Nathan, like Luke, was highly motivated by financial success and aspired to a career in banking. Graduating with a first-class law degree, Nathan experienced a smooth transition to his desired profession. Over all the years of interviews with Nathan, he presented as very focused and strategic in his career planning. During his time at university, he was acutely aware of the need to develop a strong CV and had worked hard to build his through participating in extra-curricular activities, including taking on a leadership role in the UoB's Finance Society. By the end of his second year at university, Nathan had secured an internship in a top multinational bank, which he undertook, subsequently receiving an offer of a job within the company, based in London. In his first year as a graduate, he was earning roughly £80,000 with bonuses.

From this point on, he began to be headhunted in a manner that indicates the extent to which he was a fish in water in the elite London labour market. His ready 'fit' into this milieu meant the generation of social capital that then opened up a world of opportunities:

> '[T]he job market for people with two to three years of banking experience is ridiculously hot. You know, I would typically get maybe an email or two in a week for potential jobs. So, there's loads of stuff out there and especially if you're … it's not a very big industry, there may be a couple of hundred people who do the kind of thing that we do in London, and so once you have a little bit of a reputation or some people have worked with you on a couple of deals, they start thinking, 'Oh, this guy might be alright' … so you start to get invites from headhunters, generic ones and also ones that people have referred you for.'

While it was the security of a highly paid job alongside a salary advance that were crucial in facilitating Nathan's move to London, his path was smoothed through a habitus that was completely in tune with the milieu into which he located, alongside the generation and mobilization of highly valuable social capital, both at university and in the London employment market.

Not all UoB graduates are able to reap the same rewards, and Zoe's narrative exemplifies a very different experience. Zoe was a white, working-class woman from Wales, and her transition post-graduation was much more fragmented, precarious and convoluted than the other participants discussed in this chapter. She had limited inherited or acquired economic or social capital to draw upon, which had consequences for the temporal and mobility aspects of her transition. Zoe was a young woman who was never entirely sure which path she wanted to follow in life, holding various dreams and aspirations. She gained a place to study law at the UoB and operated with a firm belief that a law degree from a Russell Group university, and work experience in 'the real world' (as opposed to undertaking unpaid internships in law companies), would provide the edge she needed for success on the graduate labour market. When she graduated, Zoe had a number of career aspirations. She settled on law because it linked to her degree and she perceived it to be the most risk-free pathway to a secure future. Zoe had an idealized vision of London as the place that she had to be, but there was no evidence that she was developing the capacity to 'fit in' to the milieu of the elite London labour market. She herself focused on how she did not have the economic resources to gain access to opportunities in London, referring to unpaid internships and work experience, which she described as out of reach:

> 'I'd have loved to have done, like, the internships and stuff, the unpaid internships in London, but I can't afford to live there because my parents don't have any money and I struggled through uni anyway. I'd have loved to have done those to gain the experience, to gain the training contracts or the vocational placements, but obviously, I didn't have that, and you need to have the money to do the work experience to get the experience to get the job that you want. And that is the catch-22.'

Unable to visualize professional employment beyond an image of working in London, she returned to her family home in Wales on graduation, hoping to find work there and build experience to support her in accessing a graduate employment scheme. However, she found herself faced with a static labour market in her local area and discussed how the 'Bristol Brand' had little currency there. Zoe deemed moving to London as the only way to achieve a successful career and appeared unable to work out how she might otherwise mobilize the cultural capital bestowed on her by her Russell Group degree. In one interview, Zoe described feeling as though she was stuck between a rock and a hard place. She talked of being headhunted by recruitment agencies in London but explained that she did not have the economic capital to enable her to take the risk of moving to the city:

> 'Recruitment consultants would ring me up and say, "Do you want to do this sales job in London", so it's not like I couldn't have got that. Because they see the CV and they know: Bristol, 2:1, law – tick. You know, it's that kind of thing, they want you, but then obviously, I didn't have the money to move to London in the first place to go and chase a job like that to then find another job in something that I wanted to do. So, it's very, really, really static in Wales because I'm still fully overdrawn now, my parents haven't got a penny to give me, they are struggling themselves, so, you know, without working for a long time in a job for crap money in Wales, I can't even generate enough money to save for a deposit, let alone anything else in London for crazy prices, for a job that I don't even want to do. So, it's really, really difficult.'

Clearly, a lack of economic capital made a move to London too much of a risk to take. However, alongside this, it was apparent that her habitus would not enable her to easily move and 'fit in' to the elite metropolitan vortex of London. Even when faced with the opportunity to take up employment in London, she was disposed to remain within the comfort zone of her home town.

She eventually managed to find what she described as a well-paid 'London job' as a legal taxonomist for a company based in London but where she could stay in Wales and work from home. This seemed to suit Zoe and her situation perfectly; however, the job itself was only temporary. Like Freya earlier in this chapter, Zoe described employing a strategy of attempting to turn this opportunity into a permanent position through "convincing" management of her value. However, unlike Freya, Zoe was unsuccessful in this endeavour and was unable to demonstrate her 'value' in the same way. In our last interview with Zoe, her temporary position was coming to an end and she was yet to find her 'place' in a career she desired or one that would reap the economic rewards to be hoped for in a graduate profession.

Conclusion

This chapter has focused on graduate labour markets in London. Using the narratives of four graduates from the Russell Group UoB, the chapter has explored what enables or constrains young graduates in gaining access to careers in the capital city. While a degree from one of the Russell Group universities functions as an important mobilizing agent, and a London home acts as a key form of capital, this chapter demonstrates that these factors alone are not enough. They work alongside other, less tangible or easily acquired dispositions and orientations, what we have called a 'London habitus', which is generated out of economic, cultural and geographical capital, alongside an associated cosmopolitanism and global acumen. The narratives in the chapter point to how, for those from more privileged backgrounds, these resources and practices are anchored in the body, that is, in a habitus that involves a taken-for-granted sense of 'fit' with what Cunningham and Savage (2015) refer to as a distinctive metropolitan elite, which builds on socially ingrained confidence and a sense of entitlement. Therefore, while policy actors commonly assume that access to elite universities offers disadvantaged students a 'boost' in gaining access to elite professions, this chapter demonstrates that not all graduates are equally able to embody and capitalize upon the symbolic value of the 'Bristol Brand'. Mobilizing the cultural capital bestowed through a stamp from the Russell Group relies on access to other forms of capital – including access to London – and is then facilitated through a habitus that is attuned to the distinctive metropolitan elite of London. We therefore conclude that attempts to address the inequalities that privilege bestows in these processes need to recognize and challenge the social magic, or social alchemy, that transforms highly prized capitals into the legitimate and deserved possessions of the advantaged middle class. Furthermore, achieving change needs to address how this process of social magic involves the cultivation of a narrative of meritocratic legitimacy among the successful (Sandel, 2020) and a misplaced belief among all that inequalities of outcome are fair (Mijs, 2019; Friedman et al, 2021).

References

Bathmaker, A.M., Ingram, N. and Waller, R. (2013) Higher education, social class and the mobilisation of capitals: recognising and playing the game, *British Journal of Sociology of Education*, 34(5/6): 723–43.

Bourdieu, P. (1990) *The Logic of Practice*, Cambridge: Polity.

Bourdieu, P. and Wacquant, L. (1992) *An Invitation to Reflexive Sociology*, Cambridge: Polity.

Brown, P. (2013) Education, opportunity and the prospects for social mobility, *British Journal of Sociology of Education*, 34(5–6): 678–700.

Cook, A.C.G., Faulconbridge, J.R. and Muzio, A. (2012) London's legal elite: recruitment through cultural capital and the reproduction of social exclusivity in City professional service fields, *Environment and Planning A*, 44(7): 1744–62.

Cunningham, N. and Savage, M. (2015) The secret garden? Elite metropolitan geographies in the UK, *Sociological Review*, 63(2): 321–58.

Fielding, A.J. (1992) Migration and social mobility: South East England as an escalator region, *Regional Studies*, 26(1): 1–15.

Friedman, S., Laurison, D. and Macmillan, L. (2017) *Social Mobility, the Class Pay Gap and Intergenerational Worklessness: New Insights from the Labour Force Survey*, London: Social Mobility Commission.

Friedman, S., O'Brien, D. and McDonald, I. (2021) Deflecting privilege: class identity and the intergenerational self, *Sociology*, 55(4): 716–33.

Igarashi, H. and Saito, H. (2014) Cosmopolitanism as cultural capital: exploring the intersection of globalization, education and stratification, *Cultural Sociology*, 8(3): 222–39.

Ingram, N. and Allen, K. (2019) 'Talent-spotting' or 'social magic'? Inequality, cultural sorting and constructions of the ideal graduate in elite professions, *The Sociological Review*, 67(3): 723–40.

Mijs, J. (2019) The paradox of inequality: income inequality and belief in meritocracy go hand in hand, *Socio-Economic Review*, 39, https://doi.org/10.1093/ser/mwy051

Oakley, K., Laurison, D., O'Brien, D. and Friedman, S. (2017) Cultural capital: arts graduates, spatial inequality, and London's impact on cultural labor markets, *American Behavioral Scientist*, 61(12): 1510–31.

Sandel, M. (2020) *The Tyranny of Merit: What's Become of the Common Good?*, London: Allen Lane.

Social Mobility Commission (2016) The social mobility index, https:// assets.publishing.service.gov.uk/government/uploads/system/uplo ads/attachment_data/file/496103/Social_Mobility_Index.pdf

Social Mobility Commission (2019) State of the nation 2018–19: social mobility in Great Britain, https://assets.publishing.service.gov.uk/ government/uploads/system/uploads/attachment_data/file/798404/ SMC_State_of_the_Nation_Report_2018-19.pdf

4

'There's No Place Like Home': Graduate Mobilities and Spatial Belonging

Introduction

This chapter focuses on the significance of 'home' for graduate mobility and the ways in which home contributes to capacities to navigate graduate futures. For young people who participate in higher education in England, the dominant narrative is one of leaving behind the family home and becoming geographically mobile. The 'student experience' is structured around a normative assumption of moving away to live in student accommodation and become immersed in university life (Patiniotis and Holdsworth, 2005; Christie, 2007; Holdsworth, 2009), despite the considerable number of students who do not leave the parental or guardian home to attend university (HESA, 2021). On completion of higher education study, there has been a similar normative expectation that graduates should be self-reliant and readily move away from their home place to locations where high-skilled work is situated (Christie and Burke, 2021). Yet, recent research indicates that it is those from privileged class backgrounds who move long distances for graduate employment (Hecht et al, 2020). Moreover, return migration to the parental home has recently become an accepted coping strategy for graduates from all social class backgrounds in a context of much less certain graduate futures (Sage et al, 2013; Stone et al, 2014).

The chapter examines how these dominant narratives of spatial mobility play out in the lives and experience of participants in the Paired Peers project. The project followed students studying at the two universities in Bristol from the start of their undergraduate degrees through to four years after graduation (2010–17) (for further details on methods, see Chapter 2). The two graduates at the heart of the chapter both studied English: Ruby, from a working-class background, who studied at the medium-tariff modern UWE; and Elliot, from a middle-class family background, who attended the high-ranking and prestigious UoB. English is a 'traditional' university discipline in England, which is particularly popular with young women. There is a perception that those who choose it tend to do so because of their love of literature, rather than for career reasons, though many may have aspirations towards working in the media or becoming a writer, while others aspire to teaching. Ruby and Elliot reflect these contrasting career aspirations and subsequent occupational pathways. The unfolding of their graduate lives allows us to explore the relations and intersections between various axes of advantage and disadvantage that shape their orientations to home, the resources available to them and their different capacities for spatial and social mobility as they progress from undergraduate study to graduate futures.

We start by considering recent research on graduate employment and student and graduate mobilities. We discuss the framework used for understanding the 'mobility narratives' presented in the chapter and then trace the lived experience of mobility of two young graduates: Ruby and Elliot. In presenting their narratives, we focus on the ways in which their orientations to 'home' and mobility are differently shaped by the habitus and predispositions developed in their home milieu. We show how these orientations become combined with the capitals available to them as they progress through and beyond higher education, and how their capacities for mobility and capacities to navigate towards a graduate future are 'class journeys' (Trondman, 1994, cited in Wiborg, 2004: 418) marked by their different social class backgrounds.

Home, mobility and graduate employment in the 2010s

Regional economic inequalities and disparities in employment opportunities are starkly visible in the UK, such that geographical mobility is seen as key to upward social and economic mobility, and crucial to gaining access to top-level jobs (Duta and Iannelli, 2018; Social Mobility Commission, 2019, 2020b; Davenport and Zaranko, 2020). In this context, participation in higher education is seen as an opportunity for those from working-class and disadvantaged backgrounds to leave home and move away to move up (Social Mobility Commission, 2020a).

As also discussed in Chapter 3, moving away, to London in particular, is associated with the possibility of accelerated social mobility (Sage et al, 2013; Stiles, 2017), even though recent research (Friedman and Macmillan, 2017) finds that it is the middle class who reap the most benefits from the capital's role as an 'escalator' region (Fielding, 1992). Nevertheless, London's continuing economic dominance (Social Mobility Commission, 2020b) channels higher education graduates towards London and the south-east (Sage et al, 2013). Those hoping to find work in such fields as the media, charity or financial sectors feel that they *have* to move to London because it is where the major organizations in these sectors are based (Social Mobility Commission, 2020a: 20). In contrast, students who stay or return to their home place after graduation either do not have an earnings premium relative to non-graduates or have only a modest premium in comparison to those who move away for employment (Kidd et al, 2017; Social Mobility Commission, 2020b).

Yet, despite the apparent employment advantages of spatial mobility, there is also growing evidence of *stasis*, that is, young people who do not leave their home place, as well as young people who return home following graduation (Ball, 2015; Cunningham and Christie, 2019), often to live with their parents – the so-called 'boomerang generation' (Mitchell, 2006). Specifically in the south-west of England, where the two universities in the Paired Peers project are located, a survey by the Higher Education Careers Service Unit (Ball, 2015) of the early migration practices of graduates who completed their studies at the same time as the

Paired Peers cohort found that around two in five (40.4 per cent) graduates who were employed in the region were 'loyals', that is, they had studied in their home region and remained to work in the region. Over a quarter (29.6 per cent) were 'returners', that is, graduates who returned to their home place after having been away to study.

Returning home: home as a base camp and launch pad for the future

Recent research in the fields of social geography and youth mobilities, as well as educational research, finds that return migration to both the family home and to the home place has become an acceptable strategy for young people from middle-class and working-class backgrounds in the UK and other major developed economies (Mitchell, 2006; Stone et al, 2014; Berngruber, 2015). Return migration is not just labour motivated, but rather involves social and cultural factors, including social ties and a sense of belonging, as well as financial and employment considerations (see, for example, Sage et al, 2013; Rérat, 2014, 2016; Finn, 2017a; Christie and Burke, 2021).

A study by Roberts, Noden, West and Lewis (2016) demonstrates how home can serve as a resource for moving forward, particularly for middle-class returners, whose parents have the financial means to offer support. They found that young middle-class graduates used the family home as: a base camp for exploration before settling into adulthood; a launch pad for careers; a savings bank, in particular, for future property purchases; a refuge for respite and reflection; and a preferred residence, whether on account of comfort, cultural practice or to support parents.

In contrast, *staying* home among the working class has acquired connotations of defeat, fixity and failure (Skeggs, 2004; Allen and Hollingworth, 2013). Those who stay in the home place are considered to have 'failed' to leave or have been 'left behind' (O'Shea et al, 2019: 7). A 'place-specific habitus' and 'stickiness' to local place (Allen and Hollingworth, 2013: 499, 502) are considered to restrict mobility. However, such normative assumptions are called into question by these and other researchers who debate how attachment to home place can be a resource not only for the advantaged, but also for those from working-class backgrounds.

Staying home: redefining home as a resource

Research in Denmark (Mærsk et al, 2021) proposes that immobility should be (re)framed as an advantageous, beneficial and deliberate strategy for some young adults because it allows them to mobilize capitals and capacities that are specific to 'insiders'. These include local job experience, knowledge about firms and organizations locally, and living with parents, alongside the capacity to achieve a desired future based on a belief in future job opportunities locally and satisfaction with social life in the local area. Henderson (2021: 186) refers to these advantages of staying in the home place as 'local' capital: 'a rich embeddedness in place that opens future possibilities and opportunities in that place'. She cautions, however, that local capital requires structural conditions and opportunities for employment locally for desired graduate futures to be realizable.

Other research emphasizes the emotional and relational importance of home. O'Shea et al (2019) discuss the complex emotional nature of decisions made about university and future lives in their study of young people in rural Australia, where leaving involves the risks of losing connection to family and the home place. Finn's (2017a) study of university-to-work transitions in the UK addresses similar concerns about the importance of kin and non-kin relationships for the ways in which graduates experience and make choices about employment and careers. Her research shows how the process of securing work and committing to a career is embedded within broader experiences of personal life, emotion and (im)mobility. Home and staying in the home place can therefore act as a spatial resource and, particularly for those from working-class backgrounds, provide a strategy for minimizing financially, socially and culturally 'risky' transitions into higher education and beyond (Clayton et al, 2009).

Habitus, capitals and capacities for mobility

In the research discussed earlier, the dominant narrative of leaving home behind is rewritten for students and graduates from both middle-class and working-class backgrounds. In order to pursue what this possible reframing of understandings of home and mobility can mean in practice, we use a framework that focuses on the role of *habitus*, *capitals* and *capacities* for mobility, and the ways in which they enable or constrain the navigation of future pathways for graduates from different social class backgrounds.

Habitus

Bourdieu's concept of habitus encapsulates how the past comes to be embodied in the present (Allen and Hollingworth, 2013: 507). It 'designates a way of being, a habitual state (especially of the body) and, in particular, a predisposition, tendency, propensity or inclination' (Bourdieu, 1984: 562). As a result, 'some courses of action are excluded from young people's "plausibility structures" (Skeggs 2004) as "unthinkable" and undesirable' (Allen and Hollingworth, 2013: 500). The concept of habitus has therefore been criticized for being deterministic, emphasizing a habitual state that locks people into particular actions and practices (King, 2000; Jenkins, 2002).

Against this, we share the view of researchers who understand habitus as '*predisposing* rather than *predetermining* individuals towards certain ways of behaving' (Allen and Hollingworth, 2013: 501, emphases added). Following this interpretation, habitus is a 'generative structure' (McNay, 1999: 100), permeable and responsive to other social experiences, at least to some extent. Thus, Holdsworth (2006: 499) emphasizes: 'One of the key attributes of habitus is the potential for invention, it is not that practices are determined by habitus, but that habitus helps us to know what to expect and how to respond to the unexpected.'

Habitus and spatial mobility

Holdsworth suggests that the requirement to engage in a new environment and therefore some form of spatial mobility as a student (and then graduate) demands a strategic active habitus. Abrahams and Ingram (2013: 1) describe a 'chameleon habitus', where individuals negotiate between their evolving identities as students and as graduates and their home place. This does not necessarily mean leaving the home place. The habitus may, for example, orientate some individuals to mitigate the risks of the unknown (Clayton et al, 2009) and to enjoy relations with the family (Finn, 2017b) by remaining at home as much as it may predispose others to welcome the opportunity to move away. Staying in the home place may thus be seen as 'agentic rather than as representing predisposition to immobility' (Finn, 2017b: 753). Finn (2017b: 753) therefore argues that we need 'a more nuanced account of mobility that moves beyond binaries of mobility/immobility, connected to dualistic notions of middle-class privilege and working-class disadvantage … where the habitus is either "mobility enabling" or characterised by "immobility"'.

Mobility as capital and capacity

Key here are the capacities and resources for mobility, what Kaufmann, Bergman and Joye (2004) refer to as 'motility'. They conceptualize motility as a form of capital that can be mobilized and transformed into other types of capital (such as economic, human and social capital): 'motility encompasses interdependent elements relating to access to different forms and degrees of mobility, competence to recognise and make use of access, and appropriation of a particular choice, including the option of non-action' (Kaufman et al, 2004: 750). Motility therefore involves the ways in which individuals are able to access and appropriate the capacity for socio-spatial mobility according to their circumstances. It involves having access to forms of capital that enable capacities to make decisions about spatial mobility.

To articulate the ways in which the capacity for mobility works, we find the notion of navigational capacities useful, as used by Gale and Parker (2015a, 2015b) in their research into student aspirations, and originating in the work of Appadurai (2004). In a similar way to Bourdieu (1977, 1997), whose tools of habitus and capitals point to the possibilities delineated by position in a social field, Appadurai emphasizes that the capacity to navigate the intermediary steps between past and future relies on a range of economic, social and cultural resources that are unevenly distributed among social groups (Gale and Parker, 2015a: 88), and cultural differences in the archives of experience result in different ways of navigating the future. However, Appadurai is concerned to move beyond accounts that suggest the reproduction of existing positions to consider how cultural groups pursue futures that are potentially at odds with their pasts.

Building on the work of Appadurai, Gale and Parker (2015a) use de Certeau's (2011 [2004]) notion of 'map' and 'tour' knowledge to consider how navigational capacities are associated with individuals' different positions in a particular field. Tour knowledge involves knowing one's way around a physical or social space through the direct instruction given by another, such as a tourist guide or guidebook. As with a tourist in a new city, those using tour knowledge are reliant on the strengths and limitations of the guide. They follow a predetermined route that they trust will lead them to their desired destination but do not have the archives of experience to work out stepping stones along the way, particularly if they encounter obstacles. Instead, when confronted with obstacles, the alternatives tend to be to choose another tour: to adapt their preferences from a doctor to a teacher, for example, when the demands of the former exceed their navigational capacities (Gale and Parker, 2015b: 148). In contrast, map knowledge is based on familiarity with the bigger picture. Those with map knowledge:

> have greater familiarity with the social terrain and an appreciation of the whole route they need to take to reach their destination from their point of origin. They have not just been given the map; they are the cartographers, able to create new routes and to improvise alternatives if obstacles appear in their way. (Gale and Parker, 2015b: 148)

Therefore, as with the notion of 'motility', navigational capacities involve a habitus that is attuned to the field, as well as access to resources or forms of capital that both shape and enable capacities to be mobile and to navigate a future. Gale and Parker (2015b: 148) give as an example the social networks of a graduate whose mother is a judge or whose uncle is a vice-chancellor and, through these forms of social capital, has access to understandings of the field that can inform their navigation beyond higher education in a very different way to a student who is 'first-in-family' (Gale and Parker, 2015b: 148).

In the next section, we consider the ways in which this plays out in the lives of the two graduates in this chapter (Ruby, who studied at UWE, and Elliot, who attended the UoB). Both are narratives of success, but as narratives of social and spatial mobility, they are very different, demonstrating how the capacities to be mobile and to navigate higher education and graduate futures form part of classed journeys to future lives and careers.

Ruby: choosing a suitable career path to stay local

Home, imagined futures and attachment to place: the social milieu of home

Ruby (white, working class, studied English) grew up in a small town in a rural county an hour away from Bristol. Her mother was a childminder and her father a van driver. While they encouraged her to go to university, she said that "They don't have any qualifications between them at all" (Interview 1) and she was the first in her immediate family to attend university. From the first time we met Ruby, she emphasized her attachment to her family and home place, saying: "I am very family orientated. I like being with my family" (Interview 1). She defined herself and her family as hard-working and respectable working class. She said that her parents owned a "nice house" that they had "worked for" (Interview 2), and her father had instilled a strong work ethic in her sister and herself: "We work. … If you want it, you work for it" (Interview 10).

While the family home was in what Ruby described as a working-class area, she constructed an image of her home place as a rural idyll, offering the prestige associated with 'country living' (Pederson and Gram, 2018): "I love it here, but I love the countryside more, I've grown up here. I'd only ever move if it was to somewhere in the country … because I just love the whole country-living idea" (Interview 6). She attended the local secondary school and then a nearby sixth-form college, and while she was "always sure" that she wanted to go on to university, higher education was not an automatic progression route for the young people in her social milieu. As she explained:

'My friends at home, a lot of them have jobs, and they could have gone to university, but they didn't, and I don't know whether it was the confidence, or money, or what, but they just didn't go. ... They don't have any motivation to save money to do things or have a focus, they just, sort of, think, "I'm just going to keep earning and spending money, and then that eventually, hopefully, something will, like, fall from the sky on my lap, or something", you know. They're not proactive; they don't want to do things.' (Interview 6)

She positioned herself as different to these friends, even though she too did not aim to move away. For Ruby, home was associated with resources and relationships that she valued, and represented a safe place from which to test out moving beyond traditional boundaries and into the unknown. She explained that she chose to study at UWE "because it's close to home, so I had that option if I wanted to move back I could" (Interview 1). While she moved to Bristol during her first year of undergraduate study and lived in university accommodation in order to try out "the whole [student] experience", by the end of the year, she decided to return home to live with her parents and commute to Bristol on a daily basis.

Ruby's life remained embedded at home, allowing her to maintain family and social ties, and providing security and a strong sense of belonging (Finn, 2017b; Cunningham and Christie, 2019). She had a part-time job in her home town. She played skittles with her mother, and she was a member of the darts team at the local pub. Her boyfriend, whom she met just before she started university, lived locally and was employed as a manager of a sports shop in a nearby town. Ruby saw this relationship as contributing to her capacity to aspire and navigate towards the future (Appadurai, 2004; Gale and Parker, 2015a, 2015b). Her partner was a source of support, someone who made her "more confident" to go to university and to subsequently pursue a teaching career (Interview 6). At the end of her undergraduate degree, her attachment to home was as strong as ever: "I would like to stay around this area; I'm a home bird. I love mum, dad; I've got nan, grandad; I've got my sister who lives around here; and I love the county, I think it's brilliant" (Interview 7).

Pursuing a clearly structured career pathway

Ruby told us that she had decided on her career goal early on at secondary school: "I want to teach ... it's something that I've always wanted to do actually, go to university. I knew what I wanted to do from about the age of 13" (Interview 2). As well as representing a visible and clearly mapped career pathway, teaching would allow Ruby to find graduate work in her home place, where she said that graduate opportunities and secure employment were limited: "We have quite a lot of temporary jobs. ... We have, like, Tesco [supermarket chain] and supermarkets, which, like, they're always temporary, you can never quite find anything that's sort of permanent. ... There are so many people going for one job, it is quite hard" (Interview 3). Her career goal was a way of mitigating the uncertainties and risks involved in pursuing a path that was different to the experience of her family and friends. Her hope for the future was the security of a permanent job (Interview 6).

Once at university, she dedicated her time to investing in capitals that would enhance her chances of achieving her career goal. She emphasized that she was hard-working, not distracted by student social life and kept focused on her studies in order to achieve a good degree outcome. She found work experience placements in a number of different schools during university vacations. When she came to the end of her undergraduate degree, she strategically applied for a post-graduate teacher-training programme at universities near to home in order to improve her chances of securing future employment locally. When making job applications, she made use of her immediate social networks, which included "the whole team" of tutors on her teacher education course, as well as her partner and a close friend:

> 'One of them works for the NHS [National health Service] and she's always dealing with applications, so I sent it [my application] to her as well because I thought you always need that different viewpoint of what your application sounds like. ... And then [my partner] would proofread it for me because he's so good at that.' (Interview 7)

Her tentative confidence in herself, and the importance of staying local, became very apparent in her reaction when she was offered a teaching post in the nearest town to where she lived: "When they phoned me, oh my, I was just screaming. I said, 'Are you sure? Are you sure?' She [the headteacher] went, 'Yeah'. I came off the phone and [my partner] said, 'I think they think you're mad because you were going, "Are you sure? Are you sure?"'" (Interview 7). Once in post, Ruby set about creating a life embedded in her local area. She initially continued to live with her parents, who supported her financially, so that she could save to buy a home of her own. Two years after graduating, she bought a house with her now fiancé, and she envisaged a settled future in her home place with a long-term career in teaching, working her way up from team leader or special needs coordinator to head teacher.

Elliot: complex mobilities and mapping a future of his own creation

Home, imagined futures and attachment to mobility: the social milieu of home

The social milieu of home and Elliot's orientation to family and attachment to his home place were markedly different to Ruby's. Elliot (white, middle class, studied English) grew up in Northern Ireland. His father was a filmmaker and his mother, who stayed at home to raise the family, had previously had a career as an interior designer. Both his parents had attended university. The family moved from London to Northern Ireland when Elliot was six months old, and he grew up surrounded by family friends, who had also migrated from England and who shared a similar middle-class lifestyle:

> 'There's quite an English sensibility to the people who are there, and not many people in the circle have strong Northern Irish accents. ... The main bit of the circle was public school educated, like army people. Yes, kind of a lot of country houses and that kind of thing, yeah. A lot of them don't go to the local grammar school,

say, that kind of thing. A lot of my good friends from Northern Ireland also go, or went, to boarding school.' (Interview 1)

The shared experience of migration and only loose attachment to the geographical place of Northern Ireland among both family and family friends were compounded for Elliot when he was sent to an elite boarding school in England to complete secondary education. Boarding school forced a separation from family and home place that he would not have wished for at the time, but which developed an independence from home that made progression to university "just kind of a natural step". As he explained: "It's such a well-trodden path for people from my school", and at home, "it's just kind of been assumed that I would go to university" (Interview 1).

He welcomed the chance to move away to study: "I want to get away and do something new. … It just seems that being close to home defeats the purpose of university I think" (Interview 1). This was not a move into the unknown for Elliot. The social milieu of boarding school had prepared him for a seamless transition to university life: "I suppose [school] is kind of a small version of colleges and halls really. So, hall life is very, very similar to house life[1] really" (Interview 1).

Elliot was highly aware of the privileges he enjoyed, which enabled him to have time to enjoy life as a student and to keep plans for the future open. Where Ruby stressed hard work as the key feature of her time at university, Elliot said, "I really can't think of a better way to spend three years" (Interview 1); looking back at the end of his degree, he said that his experience of being an undergraduate was one of "just being very, very comfortable" (Interview 6), surrounded by people from a similar background to himself. As he acknowledged later, when reflecting back on university, "It's a self-selecting kind of circle of people … it is quite exclusive" (Interview 10).

---

[1] Boarding schools in England regularly have a 'house' system, where pupils are allocated to one of a number of houses within the school, similar to the Oxford and Cambridge university college system.

Creating a route to a desired career future

Nevertheless, from the start of university, Elliot had ideas for the future, contemplating either journalism or an academic career. He aspired to "make some impression in writing" (Interview 4) but remained undecided about which route to follow. In his final year, he said: "I'm going to have to choose whether to try to be academic, to do a PhD and maybe further, or throw myself into journalism and see what happens with that" (Interview 6).

While at university, he became involved in activities that would contribute to these future goals, writing film reviews for the university newspaper and building up his responsibilities so that he was running the film and TV section of the paper by his final year. He used social contacts in his local cricket club at home to secure a summer work experience placement at the Belfast office of a major UK red-top newspaper. Moreover, while he worked part-time during the term, it was for a finance magazine published by a member of his family, where he developed journalism skills, starting off by proofreading, moving on to administrative work and commissioning articles, and then writing for the magazine. The following account provides an indication of how the capacity to map your own future is made possible through being able to mobilize and then build on stocks of social and cultural capital that count in a chosen field:

Elliot: I've been given this amazing opportunity really through nepotism, I suppose. … It's just the fact that he is my cousin. … He just said, 'Do you want to write?', and I said, 'Yes, absolutely'. Because it is difficult to find people who, you know, who know about hedge funds who aren't really expensive. That's one of the other things: I'm really cheap. He got me doing five interviews. … These hedge-fund service providers. … I think they were all a bit bemused by this 20-year-old or 21-year-old coming into their offices in a badly fitting suit and asking about the financial situation over the last year.

Interviewer:	How did it go?
Elliot:	Fine. Because even if you're out of control in the interview, you know, if you don't have a feel of what's going on, you can salvage … even if it's a stupid question, you can write it into something that sounds impressive. (Interview 6)

These opportunities contributed to a complete and deep-rooted confidence in his capacities to improvise and fashion his knowledge and skills into suitable expertise, and, importantly, enabled him to develop the navigational capacities needed to achieve his career goal. With no strong ties to his home place and friends who, "like every middle-class group of people, [had] all left home and spread apart" (Interview 8), he was open to moving away and to London if he decided to pursue a career in journalism.

Whereas Ruby remained invested in her local place and did not have the resources to spend time trying out different ideas for a possible future, Elliot's life post-graduation involved a highly mobile and complex migration trajectory (Sage et al, 2013). He initially stayed in Bristol to complete a master's degree. He then briefly used home in Northern Ireland as a base, while seeking to develop a viable career in journalism. He moved to London, where he lived an itinerant life, lodging with different friends and family, "trying to keep out from under everyone's feet" (Interview 8). There, he worked in a variety of journalism-related jobs, managing and writing for a start-up sports magazine run by a family member, and working as a subeditor for a city business magazine.

After a year feeling that he was making limited progress with his career, he decided to go travelling for a while. He moved back to Belfast to stay with a friend, earning some money to travel by working as a website editor for a law firm. At the same time, he applied for a government volunteering scheme, which offered international placements linked to promoting human rights. He was successful, but when his placement was delayed, he moved back to London and took a temporary contract subediting another business magazine, while waiting to go to Ghana for three months. Following his placement, he returned to Northern Ireland and was applying for jobs and "casually running down the money I had"

(Interview 9) when he received an offer for a paid internship with the *Financial Times* in London that he had applied for prior to going to Ghana. This might appear to be a dream opportunity, but before he even started, he was offered a permanent job as the economics reporter for a newspaper in London with a big City readership. After two weeks with the *Financial Times*, he moved to this new permanent job, where he had to "self-train in economics" and said it was "a baptism of fire" (Interview 10). The pay and promotion were limited, but he had considerable responsibility and he saw the job as "a stepping stone, definitely" (Interview 10). Four years after graduation, he was settled in London – for the time being, living in a house that he shared with friends. He had no specific plan for the future, but was considering spending time outside the UK, looking for work with a publication whose politics were less orientated towards private-sector interests, as well having children at some time in the more distant future.

Class journeys and divergent meanings of home and mobility

Our focus in presenting these two narratives has been on how capacities to navigate a graduate future, including decisions about geographical mobility, are marked, though not straightforwardly determined, by social class. We selected these two narratives because they show very clearly the significance of 'home' for individuals from different social class backgrounds and the ways in which home is utilized in contrasting ways as a resource to pursue desired futures. While Elliot could be seen as demonstrating the expansive capacities for spatial mobility that build on the advantages of his class background, Ruby, from a working-class background and home milieu, combined a determination to stay home with pursuing a graduate future that moved well beyond the past experience of family and others in her home place.

In both narratives, home is important, but it holds different spatial meanings, indicating how home may be understood as not only the place where the family lives, but also an idea that involves different degrees of attachment or rootedness to a specific place (Wiborg, 2004; Fallov et al, 2013). Thus, while 'home' was closely associated with family and home place for Ruby, Elliot had learned from an early age and through necessity to understand 'home' as multiple places: Northern Ireland, boarding school, university halls and London. These different associations with home as place led to differing orientations to staying or moving away in their capacities for graduate mobility.

Ruby's career goal of becoming a teacher gave her life a meaning and purpose that did not require her to leave home and family behind. Staying in place was a basis for moving forward, not for being 'left behind'. In a similar way to the students in Clayton et al's (2009) research, her productive capacity for navigating a future meant that her life was actively *routed through*, rather than passively *rooted in*, the particular space and place of home. Elliot's complex but upward trajectory (Sage et al, 2013) was based on the agency and power of privilege, conveyed in his sense of ease and comfort and assured optimism (Forbes and Lingard, 2015) as he progressed through university and on to a graduate life and career. He was reflexively aware of the opportunities he enjoyed as a result of the stocks of social and cultural capital available to him, and how they enabled him to take advantage of London as the place of opportunity and endless possibilities (Allen and Hollingworth, 2013), in contrast to Ruby, whose chosen career was one of the few graduate opportunities in her home place.

While both Ruby and Elliot used 'home' as a basis for agency and successful mobility, their progression to graduate futures was therefore framed by the opportunity structures of their place-based mobilities, for, as noted by Pederson and Gram (2018: 628): 'Places constitute different opportunity structures, meaning that they provide different conditions and barriers that directly and indirectly provide certain opportunities for individuals, and close others off.' The narratives are also examples of the different forms of navigational capacity suggested by Gale and Parker (2015a, 2015b). However, where Gale and Parker's research emphasizes that 'tour' knowledge limits the way in which individuals are able to navigate the future and confines horizons for action to the specifics of a predetermined route, we would argue that 'tours', or structured pathways, play an important role in enabling those from working-class backgrounds, without stocks of symbolically recognized capitals, to both imagine and realize a graduate career future on their own terms. This argument challenges current discourses and expectations of flexible, adaptable graduates who are able to construct themselves as employable in any number of occupations (Bathmaker, 2021) and highlights the significance of home and locality as a potential form of valuable but misrecognized social and cultural capital for working-class graduates.

Elliot's narrative, on the other hand, provides insights into what lies behind the navigational capacities of a 'cartographer', that is, someone who is able to create their own map of a future life and career. His navigational capacities were built up since childhood, resting on a habitus developed in his family milieu, access to resources of cultural and social capital that allowed him to take time to develop his knowledge and skills, and the assured confidence in his abilities to regroup when faced with adversity and make choices between different opportunities as his career began to take off. Tracing his experience over an extended period provides an insight into how such navigational capacities are built over a long period of time and are connected to the ways in which home provides access to, as well as the capacity to mobilize, a range of resources. In both examples, it is clear that graduate futures depend on much more than simply a preparedness to move out to move on (Social Mobility Commission, 2020a).

Conclusion

The narratives presented in this chapter problematize normative assumptions and expectations about socio-spatial mobility in the context of higher education and graduate futures, and they raise challenges for taken-for-granted assumptions about young people needing to move geographically to progress in life. The desire to stay in place and the capacity to make use of the 'insider' advantages of remaining in the home place challenge the privileging of middle-class orientations to mobility, which value particular ways of being and devalue others. This points towards a fundamental problem in policies that privilege social mobility over policies that seek to promote greater equity across communities and regions. Policy with a narrow social mobility focus, in effect, encourages the outward migration of academically able youth (Donnelly and Gamsu, 2018). Movement is understood both as a geographic necessity and as essential for those who wish to access the opportunity, wealth and prestige that a university education apparently bestows (Friedman, 2014). This chapter has highlighted how successful graduate mobility may be conceived of in different ways. However, this requires not just a determination to imagine home as a place to make a future, but also the structural conditions for this to be realizable.

Acknowledgements

A report on graduate attitudes towards place and mobility in the north-west of England by Eileen Cunningham and Fiona Christie (2019) uses a similar title to this chapter, highlighting the growing interest in the ways in which 'home' provides opportunities and constraints for graduates in making a life and making a living in different regions of England.

References

Abrahams, J. and Ingram, N. (2013) The chameleon habitus: exploring local students' negotiations of multiple fields, *Sociological Research Online*, 18(4): 2, www.socresonline.org.uk/18/4/21.html

Allen, K. and Hollingworth, S. (2013) 'Sticky subjects' or 'cosmopolitan creatives'? Social class, place and urban young people's aspirations for work in the knowledge economy, *Urban Studies*, 50: 499–517.

Appadurai, A. (2004) The capacity to aspire: culture and the terms of recognition, in V. Rao and M. Walton (eds) *Culture and Public Action*, Stanford, CA: Stanford University Press, pp 59–84.

Ball, C. (2015) *Loyals, Stayers, Returners and Incomers: Graduate Migration Patterns*, Manchester: Higher Education Careers Services Unit.

Bathmaker, A.M. (2021) Constructing a graduate career future: working with Bourdieu to understand transitions from university to employment for students from working-class backgrounds in England, *European Journal of Education*, 56(1): 78–92.

Berngruber, A. (2015) 'Generation boomerang' in Germany? Returning to the parental home in young adulthood, *Journal of Youth Studies*, 18(10): 1274–90.

Bourdieu, P. (1977) *Outline of a Theory of Practice*, Cambridge: Cambridge University Press.

Bourdieu, P. (1984) *Distinction: A Social Critique of the Judgement of Taste* (trans R. Nice), London: Routledge & Kegan Paul.

Bourdieu, P. (1997) The forms of capital, in A.H. Halsey, H. Lauder, P. Brown and A. Stuart Wells (eds) *Education: Culture, Economy and Society*, Oxford: Oxford University Press, pp 46–58.

Christie, F. and Burke, C. (2021) Stories of family in working-class graduates' early careers, *British Educational Research Journal*, 47(1): 85–104.

Christie, H. (2007) Higher education and spatial (im)mobility: non-traditional students and living at home, *Environment and Planning A: Economy and Space*, 39(10): 2445–63.

Clayton, J., Crozier, G. and Reay, D. (2009) Home and away: risk, familiarity and the multiple geographies of the higher education experience, *International Studies in Sociology of Education*, 19(3–4): 157–74.

Cunningham, E. and Christie, F. (2019) *No Place Like Home: An Exploration of Graduate Attitudes toward Place and Mobility*, Bristol: Prospects Luminate, https://luminate.prospects.ac.uk/no-place-like-home-graduate-attitudes-toward-place-and-mobility

Davenport, A. and Zaranko, B. (2020) Levelling up: where and how?, in C. Emmerson, C. Farquharson and P. Johnson (eds) *IFS Green Budget 2020*, London: Institute of Fiscal Studies, pp 315–71, https://ifs.org.uk/sites/default/files/output_url_files/IFS%252520GB2020%252520Digital.pdf

De Certeau, M. (2011 [2004]) *The Practice of Everyday Life*, Los Angeles: University of California Press.

Donnelly, M. and Gamsu, S. (2018) Regional structures of feeling? A spatially and socially differentiated analysis of UK student im/mobility, *British Journal of Sociology of Education*, 39(7): 961–81.

Duta, A. and Iannelli, C. (2018) Social class inequalities in graduates' labour market outcomes: the role of spatial job opportunities, *Social Sciences*, 7(10): 1–18.

Fallov, M.A., Jørgensen, A. and Knudsen, L.B. (2013) Mobile forms of belonging, *Mobilities*, 8(4): 467–86.

Fielding, A. (1992) Migration and social mobility: South East England as an escalator region, *Regional Studies*, 26(1): 1–15.

Finn, K. (2017a) Relational transitions, emotional decisions: new directions for theorising graduate employment, *Journal of Education and Work*, 30(4): 419–31.

Finn, K. (2017b) Multiple, relational and emotional mobilities: understanding student mobilities in higher education as more than 'staying local' and 'going away', *British Educational Research Journal*, 43(4): 743–58.

Forbes, J. and Lingard, B. (2015) Assured optimism in a Scottish girls' school: habitus and the (re)production of global privilege, *British Journal of Sociology of Education*, 36(1): 116–36.

Friedman, S. (2014) The price of the ticket: rethinking the experience of social mobility, *Sociology*, 48(2): 352–68.

Friedman, S. and Macmillan, L. (2017) Is London really the engine-room? Migration, opportunity hoarding and regional social mobility in the UK, *National Institute Economic Review*, 240(1): R58–72.

Gale, T. and Parker, S.T. (2015a) Calculating student aspiration: Bourdieu, spatiality and the politics of recognition, *Cambridge Journal of Education*, 45(1): 81–96.

Gale, T. and Parker, S.T. (2015b) To aspire: a systematic reflection on understanding aspirations in higher education, *Australian Educational Researcher*, 42(2): 139–53.

Hecht, K., McArthur, D., Savage, M. and Friedman, S. (2020) *Elites in the UK: Pulling Away? Social Mobility, Geographic Mobility and Elite Occupations*, London: Sutton Trust, www.suttontrust.com/our-research/uk-elites-pulling-away/

Henderson, H. (2021) *Non-university Higher Education: Geographies of Place, Possibility and Inequality*, London: Bloomsbury.

HESA (Higher Education Statistics Agency) (2021) Chart 4 – full-time and sandwich students by term-time accommodation: academic years 2014/15 to 2019/20, www.hesa.ac.uk/data-and-analysis/students/chart-4

Holdsworth, C. (2006) 'Don't you think you're missing out, living at home?' Student experiences and residential transitions, *The Sociological Review*, 54(3): 495–519.

Holdsworth, C. (2009) 'Going away to uni': mobility, modernity, and independence of English higher education students, *Environment and Planning A*, 41(8): 1849–64.

Jenkins, J. (2002) *Pierre Bourdieu*, London: Routledge.

Kaufmann, V., Bergman, M.M. and Joye, D. (2004). Motility: mobility as capital, *International Journal of Urban and Regional Research*, 28(4): 745–56.

Kidd, M.P., O'Leary, N. and Sloane P. (2017) The impact of mobility on early career earnings: a quantile regression approach for UK graduates, *Economic Modelling*, 62: 90–102.

King, A. (2000) Thinking with Bourdieu against Bourdieu: a 'practical' critique of the habitus, *Sociological Theory*, 18(3): 417–33.

Mærsk, E., Sørensen, J., Thuesen, A. and Haartsen, T. (2021) Staying for the benefits: location-specific insider advantages for geographically *im*mobile students in higher education, *Population Space Place*, e2442, https://doi.org/10.1002/psp.2442

McNay, L. (1999) Gender, habitus and the field: Pierre Bourdieu and the limits of reflexivity, *Theory, Culture and Society*, 16: 95–117.

Mitchell, B.A. (2006) The boomerang age from childhood to adulthood: emergent trends and issues for aging families, *Canadian Studies in Population*, 33(2): 155–78.

O'Shea, S., Southgate, E., Jardine, A. and Delahunty, J. (2019) 'Learning to leave' or 'striving to stay': considering the desires and decisions of rural young people in relation to post-schooling futures, *Emotion, Space and Society*, 32, https://doi.org/10.1016/j.emospa.2019.100587

Patiniotis, J. and Holdsworth, C. (2005) 'Seize that chance!' Leaving home and transitions to higher education, *Journal of Youth Studies*, 8(1): 81–95.

Pedersen, H.D. and Gram, M. (2018) 'The brainy ones are leaving': the subtlety of (un)cool places through the eyes of rural youth, *Journal of Youth Studies*, 21(5): 620–35.

Rérat, P. (2014) Highly qualified rural youth: why do young graduates return to their home region?, *Children's Geographies*, 12(1): 70–86.

Rérat, P. (2016) Migration and post-university transition: why do university graduates not return to their rural home region?, *Geographica Helvetica*, 71(4): 271–82.

Roberts, J., Noden, P., West, A. and Lewis, J. (2016) Living with the parents: the purpose of young graduates' return to the parental home in England, *Journal of Youth Studies*, 19(3): 319–37.

Sage, J., Evandrou, M. and Falkingham, J. (2013) Onwards or homewards? Complex graduate migration pathways, wellbeing and the 'parental safety net', *Population, Space and Place*, 19(6): 738–55.

Skeggs, B. (2004) Exchange, value and affect: Bourdieu and 'the self', *The Sociological Review*, 52(2): 75–95.

Social Mobility Commission (2019) *State of the Nation 2018–19: Social Mobility in Great Britain*, London: Social Mobility Commission, www.gov.uk/government/publications/social-mobility-in-great-britain-state-of-the-nation-2018-to-2019

Social Mobility Commission (2020a) *Moving Out to Move On: Understanding the Link between Migration, Disadvantage and Social Mobility*, London: Social Mobility Commission, www.gov.uk/government/publications/internal-migration-and-social-mobility-moving-out-to-move-on

Social Mobility Commission (2020b) *Monitoring Social Mobility, 2013–2020: Is the Government Delivering on Our Recommendations?*, London: Social Mobility Commission, www.gov.uk/government/publications/monitoring-social-mobility-2013-to-2020

Stiles, A. (2017) *Escalator Regions in the 21st Century: Examining the Relationship between Social Mobility and Internal Migration within England and Wales during Recent Decades*, UCL Migration Research Unit Working Paper 2017/4, London: University College London, www.geog.ucl.ac.uk/research/research-centres/migration-research-unit/publications/working-papers

Stone, J., Berrington, A. and Falkingham, J. (2014) Gender, turning points, and boomerangs: returning home in young adulthood in Great Britain, *Demography*, 51(1): 257–76.

Wiborg, A. (2004) Place, nature and migration: students' attachment to their rural home places, *Sociologia Ruralis*, 44(4): 416–32.

Jobs for the Boys?
Gender, Capital and
Male-Dominated Fields

Introduction

This chapter focuses on the male-dominated field of engineering and explores intersections of class and gender in relation to new graduates' experiences of trying to establish themselves in this section of the labour market. Specifically, we draw upon the work of Bourdieu and his concepts of habitus, symbolic violence and misrecognition, as well as developing an understanding of symbolically recognized capital in the engineering field, which we suggest could be seen as a form of 'engineering capital' (an extension of Bourdieu's different forms of capital), to help us examine how and why young women access, participate in but then leave the field of engineering, while young men are supported to succeed. We start the chapter by locating the experience of those who studied engineering in the context of other participants in the Paired Peers study, showing how the graduate outcomes of most of the Paired Peers participants followed gendered patterns.

Different gender, different career aspirations and outcomes

The majority of young women in our study opted for female-dominated professions, such as teaching, administration and charity

Table 5.1: Participants by occupation and gender at Interview 10, three-and-a-half years after graduation

Occupation	Female	Male	Total
Finance/accounting/economics	2	7	9
Law	1	2	3
Teaching	8	2	10
Engineering	4	2	6
Charity/third sector	5	1	6
Office/administration	3	1	4
Public sector	1	2	3
Further education	3	2	5
Editing/journalism	3	1	4
IT	1	1	2
Other	0	1	1

work (see Table 5.1). This included a number of female graduates who started with aspirations in traditionally male-dominated professions like law but opted out and switched to teaching. They said that they did so for the perceived compatibility of their chosen employment with motherhood, following the patterns found in other research of women choosing careers that reduce the likelihood of discrimination and are more 'family-friendly' (Chevallier, 2007).

The patterns of graduate career progression that we found among the participants in Phase 2 of our research could be seen to reflect understandings of the process of developing a career identity, where the way in which 'individuals consciously link their own interests, motivations and competencies with acceptable career roles' is considered to begin in childhood and is further developed throughout an agent's life course (Praskova et al, 2015: 145). Young children have been found to 'identify caring tasks with women, machines and technology with men', and as they begin to consider future career selves, few people stray from these and other hegemonic gendered ideas of what is considered a 'suitable' career for the 'likes of them' (Bradley, 2015: 111). Not only do these gendered ideas inform what is considered 'suitable', but they also play a role in what young people consider 'worthwhile' and 'desirable' (Archer and Leathwood, 2003).

As shown in Table 5.1, not all young women follow these gendered patterns of career decision making. In this chapter, we focus on the field of engineering, a traditionally male-dominated sector. We consider the experience of two engineering graduates, both of whom studied at the UoB: Jennifer (a white, middle-class female), who graduated with a first-class degree; and Marcus (a white, working-class male), who graduated with a 2:1. We explore the process whereby Jennifer, despite having the benefits of studying abroad for a year, achieving a higher degree classification and having the capacity to draw on various forms of capitals unavailable to Marcus, graduated to a waitressing job on the minimum wage with a zero-hours contract, while Marcus immediately progressed onto a prestigious graduate engineering scheme. These two young graduates provide an insight into how gender intersects with social class in the process of achieving graduate careers, challenging an account that only considers social class inequality.

The (gendered) field of engineering

Professions like engineering could be argued to act as a 'field', as they are a social space structured according to different types and amounts of capital (Bourdieu and Wacquant, 1992), and regulate access through 'tacit requirements, such as age, sex, social or ethnic origin, overtly or implicitly guiding co-option choices … so that members of the corps who lack these traits are excluded or marginalised' (Bourdieu, 1984: 103). In the case of engineering, gender appears to be a central 'tacit requirement'. Engineering has traditionally been seen as 'male', tough, rational and somewhat uncreative, and thus unsuitable for women (Evetts, 1998; Faulkner, 2009; Powell et al, 2009; Hatmaker, 2013). The male-dominated character of the profession starts at the stage of undergraduate study, as noted by female engineering students in our cohort: "I do engineering, so, like, I'm outnumbered ten to one by guys" (Lizzie, second-year engineering student, UoB, Interview 3); and "I'm one of only, like, nine women out of a hundred and something men on my course" (Amber, second-year engineering student, UWE, Interview 4). The association of the engineering field with 'male' plays out in a male–female opposition that then shapes practices in employment (Bourdieu, 2001: 30). This includes such obstacles as stereotyping, bias and a lack of opportunities to work on a flexible basis to meet the needs of motherhood and caring responsibilities (Durbin and Tomlinson, 2010; Institution of Engineering and Technology, 2017; Papafilippou and Bentley, 2017). It is further reinforced by workplace cultures. These include apparently harmless conversations between colleagues around typically masculine topics, such as sports (Faulkner, 2009), which can lead women to feel isolated and excluded (Watts, 2009). However, they also involve sexualized and sexist jokes that work to undermine women by emphasizing that women are inferior and do not really 'belong' (McLean et al, 1997). As Holmes (2000) notes, humour can be used to emphasize or reinforce power relationships. It is a means of embedding unacceptable behaviour in superficially harmless statements, thus allowing the dominant figure to maintain authority while continuing to appear friendly.

These gendered norms are secured and seen as 'normal' through the internalization and embodiment of such structures in the dispositions and habitus of actors (McLeod, 2005). Bourdieu (2001) defines this process as 'symbolic violence', that is, 'violence which is exercised upon a social agent with his or her complicity' (Bourdieu, 1992: 167). Here, women tend to misrecognize their domination, as their sexually differentiated dispositions, or their gendered habitus, lead them 'to take the point of view of the dominant on the dominant and on themselves' (Bourdieu, 2001: 41).

'Engineering capital': symbolically recognized capital in the engineering field

As indicated earlier, social fields are differentiated by gender (as well as by class and race), as the habitus is a result of different relations of power, identity positions and the unequal distribution of capitals: economic, cultural, social and symbolic (Skeggs, 1997). For Bourdieu (1984: 315–16), capital goes some way to determine the 'position in the power relations constituting the field of power and also determines the strategies available for use in these struggles', and is thus key to social reproduction. However, as McCall (1992) highlights, gender could be considered a hidden and universal form of cultural capital through which different value is bestowed on different genders.

In exploring why engineering remains a male-dominated field and struggles to attract and retain women, we employ Bourdieu's concept of capital. We suggest that there are specific forms of symbolically recognized capital in the engineering field that combine to operate as a form of 'engineering capital'. We take inspiration for this from Archer et al's (2012, 2014) work on 'science capital'. 'Science capital' was conceptualized with the aim of understanding how 'families (and their values, resources, sense of "self"/identity, and practices) may relate to children's (science) aspirations' (Archer et al, 2012: 84). The concept was developed to understand the human, cultural and social capital involved, as well as the predispositions held by young people towards science. Capital in the field of engineering can be seen in a similar way as comprising social capital (who agents know in the field of engineering and how these people can help them achieve power in the field) and cultural capital (engineering credentials, experience of cultural activities relating to engineering and engaging in tasks/games in the home that are engineering focused).

Lips (2012: 179) outlines how different forms of capital, habitus and gender are intertwined to influence success in the field of employment:

> For human capital attributes such as education, skills and experience to translate into rewards, those attributes must be recognized and appreciated by colleagues, supervisors, and potential employers – and this recognition and appreciation depends significantly on the individual's connections with and image among other people. Gender, through stereotypes, norms and expectations, affects relationships and thus cannot but affect social capital.

Marcus: being the right person in the right place in the field of engineering

Marcus came from a working-class background and was the first in his family to go to university. Growing up, he shared a passion for motors with his father, and they bonded over this shared interest by attending different cultural events, such as car shows, together. His father encouraged and facilitated Marcus's participation in such cultural activities from a young age, and this provided him with the opportunity to begin developing engineering capital as a young boy, which would later enable him to 'fit in' to the engineering profession, to be 'as a fish in water' (Bourdieu and Wacquant, 1992: 127). The cultural activities not only satisfied his interest in engineering, but also prompted Marcus to consider engineering as a future profession. This early development of aspirations to work in engineering is key to gaining access. Tai et al (2006) found that children aged 14 with aspirations to work in engineering were 3.4 times more likely to achieve a degree in engineering compared to those without such expectations at this young age. Through establishing these aspirations early, Marcus knew at a young age that in order to access the engineering profession, he would require good grades in mathematics and physics at GCSE and A-Level:

> 'I decided to get into Engineering a long time ago, back in Year 9, and started looking at possible careers. At that point, I had a major interest in motorsport and ended up looking at different universities for motorsport and went on a summer-school course and, sort of, ended up choosing my GCSEs and A-levels with an aim towards getting into some form of engineering.' (Interview 1)

Studying engineering was Marcus's first and only choice, and as he achieved a grade A in mathematics and physics at A-Level, he had the grades to study engineering. While at university, Marcus consistently achieved good grades and graduated with a 2:1. During his studies, he undertook a summer placement within the automotive industry he had always wished to work for, gaining the work experience that is argued to be essential to gain access to the engineering profession (Brown et al, 2004). As he came to the end of undergraduate study, he was supremely confident that he would attain a successful career in engineering:

> 'My belief is there is no reason why anybody can't become the top 10 per cent of anything they want,

if you just learn and try hard, that's something that everyone can achieve. And if there's something I want, I'll find a way of getting it. It happens – as will be proved when I get an offer from [automotive engineering company] in a couple of weeks.' (Interview 6)

When asked whether he believed that the increasing rates of graduate underemployment and unemployment would affect him, Marcus replied:

'I don't think it will affect me. I'm not the kind of person to let it affect me. If I want a job, I'll go out and get a job. I've always been able to, if I've needed to work, I can go out and get a job, I've always managed to. I get decent-paid jobs for my age as well, so up until now, it's something that has not been an issue. ... No, I don't think graduate unemployment will affect me. If worst comes to worst, I'll have to play the network game, where I've met a few people over the years.' (Interview 4)

Marcus's confidence that he would not be affected by underemployment or unemployment demonstrates his level of belief in his own agency to direct his own pathway. He bases this resource of agentic capacity on both the cultural capital developed through previous jobs and the connections – the social capital – he had developed in the field of engineering employment.

Marcus concluded his studies having secured a place on a graduate scheme in the same company in which he had completed a summer placement. The clearest and most succinct summary of Marcus's career narrative is provided in his own words: "I knew what I wanted to do and did it. When it came to getting this job, I just applied for the one summer placement that I wanted and got that one, and then I got the job" (Interview 7). As a young man, he had proactively sought to develop his engineering capital in a formal sense by taking a degree in engineering and in an informal sense by participating in extra-curricular activities synonymous with the engineering field, as well as by developing social capital in the company he worked for while studying, which enabled him to progress successfully to a graduate scheme post-graduation. Through doing these things, Marcus was able to combine an abundance of relevant forms of capital over time, which enabled him to secure a smooth transition from university to employment.

Despite coming from an upper-working-class background, Marcus had felt that he fitted in and was in tune with the engineering culture at the elite university of the UoB and in the professional workplace. This is perhaps because engineering is considered to be among the most meritocratic professions in the UK (Friedman and Laurison, 2015), and his father (involved in programming) had worked with him to develop cultural capital in this area that he could then mobilize in the workplace in order to demonstrate 'value' and secure a sense of 'place':

> 'I'm involved in various other bits and similar roles in my department, so that's what I enjoy [spending time with co-workers]. In terms of work, I enjoy ... possibly my most enjoyable courses have actually been related to design and programming. Well, programming kind of runs in the family, so no surprise there.' (Interview 7)

Marcus admitted that being male and white gave him an advantage. He was well aware that "you get more men in engineering, men still dominate" and that "being British, working predominantly with other British people, does sometimes give you an advantage" (Interview 7). He sensed that the field of engineering favours those who embody the 'right' dispositions and whose bodies are not marked as strangers or invaders in a predominantly male and white space (Puwar, 2004), and therefore form a natural fit. As a result, Marcus did not experience or witness any form of discrimination. Despite acknowledging the advantages of being male and white, he nevertheless suggested that "There's a lot of things giving an advantage to women to come into engineering now, which are making it disadvantageous to be a male" (Interview 6). Once in employment, he was under the impression that there were a lot of women in his company and claimed that "the percentage of women we have in my department and in a lot of the engineering areas is considerably higher than most people imagine" (Interview 6).

These apparently contradictory views point to the effects of the 'embodied' nature of the engineering habitus, or 'the somatisation of power relations' (McNay, 1999: 104), and how these connect to ingrained perceptions of the meritocratic entitlement of the, in this case, male majority. On the one hand, Marcus was prepared to acknowledge that "We still have some of the old guard who might make the occasional cheeky jokes, etc, but there's none of that in anyone I would say who is under 40–45. … We're all engineers; we're all working for a common goal. I've never seen any animosity" (Interview 7). On the other hand, his reaction to efforts to increase the number of women in the field of engineering was that (meritocratic) power relations were being unfairly interrupted to the detriment of men.

The correspondence of Marcus's social identity and gender to the dominant social identity of the fields of engineering education and the engineering profession in the UK meant that Marcus had similar cultural capital in the form of tastes and habits, which enabled him to socialize more easily with his colleagues and seniors, and thus develop social capital in the workplace with relative ease. For example, he joined the same running club as his manager and, as a result, managed to build a strong relationship with him. Indeed, other empirical studies confirm that important informal networking in male-dominated sectors like engineering happens around taking part in, or talking about, sports (Wajcman, 1998; Charles and Aull-Davies, 2000). In Marcus's case, engaging in these activities provided him with further opportunities to develop his stock of capitals in the field. He was able to talk to his manager on an informal basis about projects at work and his own career progression, while his manager shared strategies through which the young graduate could achieve his aspirations to become a senior engineer.

In terms of career progression, Marcus spoke of his trajectory through the graduate scheme as "at a high level" and one that would lead him into management. To him, this trajectory "seems to be a natural progression" (Interview 7). As part of his graduate scheme, Marcus was allocated a mentor, with whom he was able to establish a good relationship. His mentor worked with him to strategically develop a career plan:

'And that, sort of, role is what I would like to go towards. It's management but actually of … it is still people, but it's more technical and engineering based, instead of just doing stakeholder and processes. So, I think that's the career path I'm on, and that's what my manager in my home department who is responsible for what I do and, sort of, helping develop me, that's what he's planning for me to be doing in a few years' time.' (Interview 8)

As a result of developing and mobilizing a range of capitals recognized in the field of engineering with a mentor he was in tune with, who helped with "developing" his career, and due to embodying a clear fit with the field of engineering as a white male, Marcus developed a strong sense of confidence about his career future. In the following quote, he talks about the level on which he wishes to progress from graduate trainee to full engineer:

'It's typical for you to come out on a C grade. I have declared my intentions to my manager that I want to be one of the highest C grades when I start or start on a D grade. It has been done before. … I'm relatively ambitious and would like to try and get on to the leadership level in about five years.' (Interview 7)

Indeed, as soon as Marcus finished his graduate scheme, he was considered not only for promotion to senior engineer, but also for a managerial role in another department.

Jennifer: a female space invader in the male-dominated field of engineering

Jennifer was from a middle-class family. Both her parents attended university and were teachers. Like Marcus, Jennifer had long been interested in engineering and had bonded with her father over their love for machines, particularly planes. As with Marcus, Jennifer's father influenced her decision to go into engineering by encouraging her to study the required subjects and to participate in relevant cultural activities outside of her formal education.

While at school, she developed relevant cultural and social capital by joining the Air Cadets and participating in a nationwide Engineering Education Scheme when she was in the Sixth Form (Year 12). She had strong levels of social capital within her family in the field of engineering. Her great uncle, who was a civil engineer, hosted engineering projects, which Jennifer helped with before and during her time at university: "So, sometimes, I go to, like, fairs and, like, big engineering events with them, and I guess that's quite good to be able to, sort of, talk to other people there who are interested in engineering and they might actually be in the industry" (Interview 4).

Jennifer started university with higher levels of educational credentials in mathematics and physics, as well as what appeared to be a greater level of engineering capital, than Marcus. Her aspirations upon arriving at the UoB were more specific than Marcus's, as she had already developed aspirations to work in a particular part of the engineering industry: "I definitely want to be an engineer … like, working on planes. I'd like to at a company like [aerospace company]" (Interview 1). However, unlike Marcus, Jennifer displayed lower levels of confidence in her ability to study engineering at undergraduate level; she worried that it would be "too hard", though she had passed all relevant GCSEs as well as A-Levels to a high standard (A★ in mathematics and physics, a grade higher than Marcus's A grades). While Jennifer could not have achieved a higher grade, she only described her skills in these subjects as "goodish": "I was always goodish at maths and physics and somehow wanted to apply that to planes" (Interview 2). The sense of confidence and fit that was apparent in Marcus was very different for Jennifer. Despite the apparent advantages of her social class background and a wealth of relevant cultural and social capital, her insecurities pointed to how the socially structured 'inferiority' of female engineers can become embodied and ingrained in the habitus, already visible during undergraduate study before progressing to employment.

In her second year at university, Jennifer took part in an Erasmus programme, where she spent a year studying in Spain. These 'cosmopolitan' experiences have grown more popular since 2010, as they are considered to demonstrate good 'global citizenship', a form of cultural capital that is valued by graduate employers (Snee, 2014; Ingram and Allen, 2019).

This is not an uncommon experience for middle-class undergraduate students, but one that many working-class students cannot access due to the cost (Lucey et al, 2003; Vigurs et al, 2016). Jennifer's aim in participating in the Erasmus programme was to develop a distinctive CV and to put into practice her growing ability to speak Spanish. Learning a language was a weekly extra-curricular activity she had taken part in while at university with the deliberate intention of being perceived as 'employable' in the globalized graduate labour market:

> 'It works really in your favour if you've got a language that you can speak well, and I've heard that it looks good [on your CV] if you've been away for a year. If I wasn't going to Spain, then I really would have wanted to apply for, like, an internship or something, I think that would have been really helpful.' (Interview 4)

Overall, Jennifer consistently achieved higher grades than Marcus and she graduated with a first-class honours degree. However, while she achieved a higher grade than Marcus and had taken part in extra-curricular activities and completed a year abroad, Jennifer's transition into employment was more precarious and fragmented.

During her undergraduate studies, she had regularly demonstrated an eager commitment to enter the field of engineering employment: "I'm excited about having a job and using what I've learnt and, I don't know, being in the real world" (Interview 4). As an undergraduate student, she spoke of becoming a chartered engineer, possibly doing a PhD in aerodynamics and becoming a manager in an engineering company in the future, which contrasts with findings from other research that female undergraduates struggle to see themselves in employment positions of high status after graduation (Lips, 2004).

However, on graduation, even though Jennifer managed to secure a place on two engineering graduate schemes, she struggled to see herself as an engineer: "When I graduated, I wasn't in a position to decide – well, I didn't think I was in a position to say that … oh well, you know, basically, to make my life decision" (Interview 8).

She chose to defer her place on the graduate scheme for a year and work in a pub so that she could save money to go travelling in South America, which she did. When she returned home, she continued having doubts, saying: "It's a fine job; it's just me not being sure" (Interview 8). Nevertheless, she started the graduate scheme but found the job "unfulfilling", as her first placement "didn't feel like engineering at all; it just felt like an admin job" (Interview 8). Her doubts were accentuated by feeling that she was "different" and did not 'fit in' to the workplace: "When you first go to work and it's like that, 'OK, everyone's not like me', but once you've been there for a bit, like a while, you sort of, I don't know, you get used to it" (Interview 8). Like Marcus, she was allocated a mentor. However, while Marcus enjoyed a beneficial relationship with his mentor, Jennifer's left and was not replaced:

> 'I started off with a different mentor who was really, really good and was a woman, and then she left and I was really sad because, like, she was just so good. I just found her very inspiring and, like, I don't know, she was always good. ... But then she left – super annoying. Now, my home team manager is ... no he's not really my mentor; he's just my manager.' (Interview 10)

In the male-dominated world of engineering, the importance of a mentor who could provide the crucial support, acceptance, exposure and encouragement needed to develop a career (Durbin, 2010; Durbin and Tomlinson, 2014; Lopes et al, 2015) was very apparent. When her mentor was not replaced, Jennifer began to struggle to imagine a clear career direction. Nevertheless, she looked for other female engineers in her company to find inspiration for her career:

> 'One of the managers at [automotive company], I think she's only been working there for a few years, but she did something different before and, like, she got her PhD. ... I always, like, admire people that have got PhDs and then are also high up in industry. It's, like, "OK, you're clever and you're in that position", like that's ... I always, like, admire that. So, she's got a PhD, she is, like ... you know, she's a manager in a

hugely male-dominated industry. When she goes to a meeting, there's, like, 20 men and her. And she's, like, super outdoorsy and stuff. And she gave us, like, this talk, like, when we first started, sort of, like, about her experiences. … She's just, like, this ridiculous woman that, like, can just do everything, you know. I think she's quite inspiring. And she's in the position that I hypothetically could be in.' (Interview 10)

Unlike Marcus, Jennifer found it difficult to feel part of the workplace culture and feel a sense of 'fit' due to the strongly structured and embodied hierarchical oppositions of difference, and the binary oppositions of male and female, in engineering (Skeggs, 2004). As opposed to being "the standard" (as Marcus referred to himself), Jennifer struggled to deal with being "different", with being a minority in the workplace: "People remember you more just because you are one of not many women compared to a lot of men, you're more different" (Interview 10). Jennifer described the company as "a sea of men, and most of them are white middle aged", and commented with disappointment on the gender composition of the company:

'It is a bit sad really that it's like that, especially when, like, you start. I mean they [automotive company] pride themselves on sort of having a relatively good amount of female engineers for the industry. It's, like, the industry standard is, like, 9 per cent women or something, and they've got 12 per cent, and so it's, like [sarcasm], "Oh, wow, go you!", like, 3 per cent more.' (Interview 10)

Rather than actively seeking to socialize with managers, as Marcus did, Jennifer socialized with other female colleagues, who were on a similar level to her in the organizational hierarchy. Their social interactions involved coping strategies, rather than opportunities to promote their careers:

'You just, sort of, latch on to your female friends a bit more, sort of, meet each other a bit more, have a bit of a bitch about whatever's happened over stuff. And, like, we always get really annoyed when … like, you know, a lot of emails, when sent to lots of people, will be, like, addressed, like, "Gents …", or something, and it's, like, "Piss off!", how hard is it to just say, "Hey, hi all".' (Interview 10)

The work that Marcus and Jennifer were allocated appeared to differ in importance. Many of the tasks that Jennifer engaged in upon beginning her graduate scheme were what she described as "admin", and she reported that many of the tasks she was allocated, such as simple coding or administrative tasks, were not challenging or held little responsibility. In contrast to Marcus, who was acknowledged for his qualities and skills, and was given opportunities to manage projects during his graduate scheme placement, Jennifer felt that she had to fight to make her voice heard: "I'm not sure if someone's not acknowledging what you're saying because, you know, you're new, or because you're a woman, or because you're not saying it assertively enough, or whatever" (Interview 10). Once more, Jennifer felt that it was her responsibility to change: to become 'more assertive'; to remain there for longer in order to assume more responsibilities; and to put up with conditions that would seem intolerable to others. Rather than attributing the problem to the company, lack of guidance from an absent mentor and the wrong choice of 'home department', Jennifer criticized herself: "I didn't know where in the company I wanted to be, like, there wasn't really anyone's job who I wanted, who I sort of aspired to. But, I mean, like, that might have just been my lack of company knowledge to be honest" (Interview 9). She eventually decided to apply for a different graduate scheme. She moved to the same company as Marcus, but starting out at a lower level and on a lower wage, while Marcus had already progressed up in the firm.

What we can see in the preceding excerpts from Jennifer's narrative are instances of what Bourdieu refers to as 'symbolic violence'. There is a misrecognition of Jennifer's capital, as well as a sense of complicity on her part in enacting and reproducing the social order, while being unable to recognize or fully articulate the injustice done to her (Bourdieu, 1990; Bourdieu and Wacquant,

1992). Symbolic violence meant not being given the opportunity to make an effective contribution at work, but Jennifer did not perceive it as such, and she appeared to view her situation as the *natural* order of things (Bourdieu, 1992; Webb et al, 2002).

Conclusion

While social class background has been found to play an important role in distributing graduate opportunities, with middle-class graduates much more likely to access graduate-level employment post-graduation (Burke, 2016; Friedman and Laurison, 2019), the narratives presented here provide instances of how gender intersects with class in such fields as engineering and how, in terms of successful career progression, gender can outweigh class. As the two contrasting narratives indicate, Jennifer struggled significantly more with embodying, displaying and mobilizing the stocks of valued capital that she possessed in the field of engineering due to her 'lack of fit' in the field. Marcus, on the other hand, experienced from the beginning a strong sense of fit, and upon graduation, he was confident he would achieve success. Marcus, as a white male, appeared freer to embody his engineering capital, a process less readily available to women in the engineering field, while Jennifer's engineering capital was perceived as less valuable than that of Marcus. While Marcus was supported and encouraged throughout his graduate scheme by his managers and colleagues, given challenging tasks, and offered a promotion before finishing the scheme, Jennifer struggled to make herself heard and did not find the same level of support. Instead, she found herself facing symbolic violence through others in the engineering field misrecognizing the value of her engineering capital. Further, she then put the blame on herself for not 'fitting in'.

While Jennifer did not experience overt sexism, discriminatory practices were covert yet powerful, being not only manifested in the opportunities she was given, such as low-level administration and simple coding, but also reflected in her colleagues' humour and taken-for-granted everyday practices, such as addressing emails to 'gents'. All these experiences challenged Jennifer's confidence, and as indicated in other research, confidence plays an important role in enabling women engineers to persist in the industry

(Ayre et al, 2013; Fernando et al, 2018). As a result, Jennifer struggled to see a 'clear' career pathway for herself in the engineering field.

Overall, the two cases have shown the processes by which gendered cultures and practices affect the possibility of making successful careers in particular fields, such as engineering. Even where young women may develop relevant capitals early on in their lives and establish a positive disposition towards engineering, subsequently experiencing a sense that they are 'a fish out of water' in the field means that they are less likely to be able to maintain their vision and goal of career success. The chapter has highlighted how the pressure placed on individuals to make their own futures and take responsibility for their own success is shaped and limited by the conditions and cultures in which they study and then work.

References

Archer, L. and Leathwood, C. (2003) New times – old inequalities: diverse working-class femininities in education, *Gender and Education*, 15(3): 227–35.

Archer, L., DeWitt, J., Osborne, J., Dillon, J., Willis, B. and Wong, B. (2012) Science aspirations and family habitus: how families shape children's engagement and identification with science, *American Educational Research Journal*, 49(5): 881–908.

Archer, L., Dewitt, J. and Willis, B. (2014) 'Adolescent boys' science aspirations: masculinity, capital and power, *Journal of Research in Science Teaching*, 51(1): 1–30.

Ayre, M., Mills, J. and Gill, J. (2013) 'Yes, I do belong': the women who stay in engineering, *Engineering Studies*, 5(3): 216–32.

Bourdieu, P. (1984) *Distinction: A Social Critique of the Judgment of Taste*, London: Routledge.

Bourdieu, P. (1990) *The Logic of Practice*, Cambridge: Polity.

Bourdieu, P. (1992) The purpose of reflexive sociology (the Chicago workshop), in P. Bourdieu and L. Wacquant (eds) *An Invitation to Reflexive Sociology*, Cambridge: Polity, pp 61–217.

Bourdieu, P. (2001) *Masculine Domination*, Cambridge: Polity.

Bourdieu, P. and Wacquant, L. (1992) *An Invitation to Reflexive Sociology*, Chicago, IL: University of Chicago Press.

Bradley, H. (2015) *Fractured Identities: Changing Patterns of Inequality* (2nd edn), Cambridge: Polity.

Brown, P., Hesketh, A. and Williams, S. (2004) *The Mismanagement of Talent: Employability and Jobs in the Knowledge Economy*, Oxford: Oxford University Press.

Burke, C. (2016) *Culture, Capitals and Graduate Futures: Degrees of Class*, Abingdon: Routledge.

Charles, N. and Aull-Davies, C. (2000) Cultural stereotypes and the gendering of senior management, *The Sociological Review*, 48(4): 544–69.

Chevallier, A. (2007) Education, occupation and career expectations: determinants of the gender pay gap for UK graduates, *Oxford Bulletin of Economics and Statistics*, 69(6): 819–42.

Durbin, S. (2010) SET women and careers: a case study of senior female scientists in the UK, in A. Carter-Steel and E. Carter (eds) *Women in Engineering, Science and Technology: Education and Career Challenges*, Hershey: IGI Global, pp 232–54.

Durbin, S. and Tomlinson, J. (2010) Female part-time managers: networks and career mobility, *Work, Employment and Society*, 24(4): 621–40.

Durbin, S. and Tomlinson, J. (2014) Female part-time managers: careers, mentors and role models, *Gender, Work and Organization*, 21(4): 308–20.

Evetts, J. (1998) Managing the technology but not the organization: women and career in engineering, *Women in Management Review*, 13(8): 283–90.

Faulkner, W. (2009) Doing gender in engineering workplace cultures II: gender in/authenticity and the in/visibility paradox, *Engineering Studies*, 1(3): 169–89.

Fernando, D., Cohen, L. and Duberley, J. (2018) What helps? Women engineers' accounts of staying on, *Human Resource Management Journal*, 28(3): 479–95.

Friedman, S. and Laurison, D. (2015) Introducing the 'class' ceiling, https://blogs.lse.ac.uk/politicsandpolicy/introducing-the-class-ceiling/

Friedman, S. and Laurison, D. (2019) *The Class Ceiling: Why It Pays to Be Privileged*, Cambridge: Polity.

Hatmaker, D.M. (2013) Engineering identity: gender and professional identity negotiation among women engineers, *Gender, Work & Organization*, 20(4): 382–96.

Holmes, J. (2000) Politeness, power and provocation: how humour functions in the workplace, *Discourse Studies*, 2(2): 159–85.

Ingram, N. and Allen, K. (2019) 'Talent-spotting' or 'social magic'? Inequality, cultural sorting and constructions of the ideal graduate in elite professions, *The Sociological Review*, 67(3): 723–40.

Institution of Engineering and Technology (2017) *Skills and Demands in Industry*, London: Institution of Engineering and Technology.

Lips, H. (2004) The gender gap in possible selves: divergence in academic self-views among high school and university students, *Sex Roles*, 50(5–6): 357–71.

Lips, H. (2012) The gender pay gap: challenging the rationalizations – perceived equity, discrimination, and the limits of human capital models, *Sex Roles*, 68(3–4): 169–85.

Lopes, A., Durbin, S., Neugebauer, J. and Warren, S. (2015) Mentoring professional women in aviation and aerospace, *CESR Review*, http://eprints.uwe.ac.uk/25240

Lucey, H., Melody, J. and Walkerdine, V. (2003) Uneasy hybrids: psychosocial aspects of becoming educationally successful for working-class young women, *Gender and Education*, 15(3): 285–99.

McCall, L. (1992) Does gender *fit*? Bourdieu, feminism, and conceptions of social order, *Theory and Society*, 21(6): 837–67.

McLean, C., Lewis, S., Copeland, J., Lintern, S. and O'Neill, B. (1997) Masculinity and the culture of engineering, *Australian Journal of Engineering Education*, 7(2): 143–56.

McLeod, J. (2005) Feminists re-reading Bourdieu: old debates and new questions about gender, habitus and gender change, *Theory and Research in Education*, 3(1): 11–30.

McNay, L. (1999) Agency and experience: gender as a lived relation, *The Sociological Review*, 52(2): 175–90.

Papafilippou, V. and Bentley, L. (2017) Gendered transitions, career identities and possible selves: the case of engineering graduates, *Journal of Education and Work*, 30(8): 827–39.

Powell, A., Bagilhole, B. and Dainty, A. (2009) How women engineers do and undo gender: consequences for gender equality, *Gender, Work and Organization*, 16(4): 411–28.

Praskova, A., Creed, P.A. and Hood, M. (2015) Career identity and the complex mediating relationships between career preparatory actions and career progress markers, *Journal of Vocational Behavior*, 87: 145–53.

Puwar, N. (2004) *Space Invaders: Race, Gender and Bodies Out of Place*, Oxford: Berg.

Skeggs, B. (1997) *Formations of Class and Gender: Becoming Respectable*, London: Sage.

Skeggs, B. (2004) Context and background: Pierre Bourdieu's analysis of class, gender and sexuality, *The Sociological Review*, 52(2): 19–33.

Snee, H. (2014) *A Cosmopolitan Journey? Difference, Distinction and Identity Work in Gap Year Travel*, Abingdon: Routledge.

Tai, R., Lui, C., Maltese, A. and Fan, X. (2006) Planning early for careers in science, *Science*, 312(5777): 1143–4.

Vigurs, K., Jones, S. and Harris, D. (2016) *Higher Fees, Higher Debts: Greater Expectations of Graduate Futures? A Research-Informed Comic* , Stoke-on-Trent: Staffordshire University.

Wajcman, J. (1998) *Managing Like a Man: Women and Men in Corporate Management*, Oxford: Blackwell.

Watts, J.H. (2009) 'Allowed into a man's world' meanings of work–life balance: perspectives of women civil engineers as 'minority' workers in construction, *Gender, Work and Organisation*, 16(1): 37–57.

Webb, J., Schirato, T. and Danaher, G. (2002) *Understanding Bourdieu*, Crows Nest: Allen and Unwin.

6

Intersections of Class and Gender in the Making of 'Top Boys' in the Finance Sector

Introduction

This chapter focuses on intersections of class and gender in the making of graduate careers in the finance sector. Finance is an industry perhaps best epitomizing hegemonic masculinity (Connell, 1995, 2000), where manhood is measured by financial success, and where both working and playing hard are de rigueur (Ingram and Waller, 2015). Working for a top City investment bank, in particular, is understood as a marker of aggressively achieved, hard-won financial success and masculine prowess. Graduate positions are fiercely competitive, one of the keenest examples of what Brown and colleagues have called 'the global war for talent' (Brown and Tannock, 2009; Brown et al, 2011).

Recruitment to elite graduate positions in such sectors as finance has increasingly focused on those from a small number of top-ranking universities (Wakeling and Savage, 2015), and the globalized nature of the neoliberal economic system has contributed to this trend (Brown et al, 2020), with 'blue chip' companies now recruiting from a global pool of talented graduates. This pattern of recruitment is a feature of the UK's financial services sector, particularly the City of London, following the 'Big Bang' financial deregulation in 1986 that allowed the electronic trading of stocks and shares, and that pushed London's financial status into a truly international world leader, rivalled only by New York.

The predominance of men in top jobs in the sector is documented in numerous reports (Metcalf and Rolfe, 2009; McDowell, 2011; Longlands, 2020; STEM Women, 2021). These highlight that despite the fact that women make up 43 per cent of the workforce in the financial services sector, they are significantly under-represented in leadership positions (STEM Women, 2021). This chapter focuses on what enables men to succeed and explores how male advantage in gaining access to high-status jobs in the sector is mediated by intersections with social class, benefiting those from middle-class backgrounds. The chapter focuses on three young male white graduates, all of whom pursued careers in finance. Nathan, who is white and from a securely middle-class background, completed a degree in law at the UoB. Harvey and Leo, both white and from a working-class background, studied economics (Harvey at the high-ranking UoB; Leo at UWE, a successful modern university). Focusing on the experience of these three young men enables us to explore the ways in which social class complicates a straightforward account of male success in the world of finance.

Despite the evidence of deeply entrenched class and gender inequalities in employment in the financial sector, discourses of education as the route to social mobility encourage young people to believe that with the right aspirations and motivation, they have the capacity to invent themselves and succeed, especially if they commit to, and plan strategically for, a career (Bowers-Brown et al, 2019). Harris (2004) argues that this emphasis on making one's own opportunities and the idea that success is due to personal effort, rather than structural circumstances, construct those that *can* as a mainstream cohort, but, in fact, they constitute a class elite from economically secure, professional and successful families. Those from lower-middle- and working-class backgrounds, particularly those who attend university, may not be at risk in the same way as those from lower-working-class and, what Harris (2004: 44) refers to as 'underclass', circumstances, but they do not enjoy the same advantages as the secure middle and upper-middle classes. In what follows, we explore the ways in which intersections between social class and gender affect the capacity to become a 'top boy' in the finance sector.

'Top girls' and 'top boys'

Feminist scholars and writers on youth masculinity have traced the changing experience and expectations placed on both young men and young women in the 21st century. McRobbie's work traces the rise of what she refers to as a 'new meritocracy' during the period of the New Labour government of 1997–2010 in the UK, with policies and a broader social discourse promoting a culture of individualism, together with a celebration of competitive values and behaviours. McRobbie (2007: 718) talks of 'top girls', highlighting how some young women became feted as 'ideal subjects of female success, exemplars of the new competitive meritocracy', with a 'manifest' and 'new found visibility'. Top girls are attributed the capacity to achieve economic prosperity on the basis of enthusiasm for work and having a career, facilitated by apparent systems of meritocratic reward (McRobbie, 2007: 725). These are the 'can-do' 'future girls' (Harris, 2004). McRobbie (2009: 58) writes that they 'find themselves charged with the requirement that they perform as economically active citizens' and 'are invited to recognise themselves as privileged subjects of social change', who are expected to achieve freedom and success.

The analysis of the changing nature of contemporary masculinities for young men in the 21st century stands in contrast to this. The influence of feminism, as outlined by Harris (2004) and McRobbie (2007), and changes in work roles resulting from the deindustrialization of the UK economy and decline of manual work throughout the 1970s and 1980s have led to a supposed 'crisis of masculinity' in the 1990s. While such writers as Anderson (2009) and McCormack (2014) have written of a 'softer', so-called 'inclusive', masculinity, with a decrease in sexism and homophobia among contemporary young men, Ingram and Waller (2014), among others, dispute this analysis, arguing instead for a more complex reality, with an essential continuing adherence to older forms of gender inequality and hierarchy. They talk of a 'repackaging' of forms of domination by men, in particular, by those from privileged class positions. Specifically, they show how middle-class men value forms of masculinity that promote an assertion of knowledge and intellectual authority, combined with an individualized focus on the male body as something to be crafted through grooming and physical exercise, whereas working-class men are drawn to forms of masculinity primarily focused on physicality and linked to the need to be a provider and a protector of others. In both cases, we can see differently shaped forms of hegemonic masculinity (Connell, 1995; Connell and Messerschmidt, 2005), but with middle-class men in particular, there is an emergence of the expectation for young men to aspire to have it all: to be both academically brilliant and to conform to masculine ideals of physical prowess. In this chapter, our focus is on what we call 'top boys', which connects with Ingram and Waller's (2014) ideas about men aspiring to have it all. We explore how gender and social class inequalities have reasserted themselves, as would-be 'top boys' seek to pursue precarious but potentially highly lucrative competitive and high-status careers in the financial services sector. We see 'top boys' as a new 21st-century form of hegemonic masculinity, where young men are grappling to maintain masculine domination through a raising of the stakes of the game and increased focus on excelling on all levels. This may partially be read as a response to increased labour market participation by women and the emergence of the 'top girl' as a figure to compete with, as well as the congested nature of the graduate labour market, as outlined in Chapter 1.

Aspirations, opportunities and capacities to become 'top boys' in the finance sector: the workings of social class

In this chapter, we explore the opportunity and capacity to become a 'top boy' using the experience of Nathan, Harvey and Leo. We start with Nathan, whose narrative provides a powerful account of consolidating middle-class advantage. Harvey's narrative is more complex. He had a clear view towards moving from his working-class background to a successful middle-class life, with all the possible pleasures that such a life might offer. Leo, also from a working-class background, was similarly in the process of 'becoming' middle class, but his key concern was to establish security in his future life, and financial security was one means of achieving this.

Nathan: consolidating class advantage

Nathan was from an established middle-class background. Both of Nathan's parents were doctors working in general practice and very well connected within their community. He attended a provincial grammar school and chose the UoB to study law because it was a "well-respected course" (Interview 1) and the degree would enable him to achieve his career aspiration of working in the City, while leaving options open if his career plan did not work out. As an undergraduate, he wrote a blog, something that was relatively rare in the early 2010s, in which he publicly outlined his approach to securing his desired career outcome. He actively set about building his CV during his time at university, knowing how competitive the graduate employment market would be, and was critical of what he considered to be the hedonistic and non-career-focused behaviour of many of his student peers. He was aware of how to acquire, enhance and mobilize various forms of capital (Bourdieu, 1986), as well as how to leverage them to best effect in order to stand out from his peers:

> 'Everyone has As at GCSEs, you've just got to try and differentiate yourself by doing something extra like Investment Society, or an internship, or do mooting. Because you see some of these people – particularly if you want to become a barrister – it's ridiculous, you see these people who, you know, run a soup kitchen in their spare time, got a first-class honours in their degree, been to Africa and saved a school from famine, you know, it's absolutely ridiculous how much they have! So, you've got to try and aim for that or try to match it, try and build up your CV because it's so competitive.' (Interview 2)

Along with the cultural capital of a top degree from a prestigious university, he explained how he utilized family resources and social connections to secure a position in the City based at London's Canary Wharf. He had a family member in a City investment bank who provided help, and he described how he constructed his CV to best effect, for example, listing work experience in an accountancy firm when, in practice, he had spent a couple of days in the office of his parents' accountant, in his words, just drinking tea and talking about golf. Nathan certainly understood 'the rules of the game' (Bourdieu, 1990; Bathmaker et al, 2013) when it came to succeeding in the hyper-competitive finance sector of the graduate careers market, following an approach that conforms to the notion of the 'top boy' as someone who works hard to maximize their performance in multiple arenas.

Nathan graduated with a first-class honours degree and moved into employment with a top investment bank. A year after graduation, Nathan was based at London's Canary Wharf, having previously spent several months in New York with his new employer. For Nathan, competition was not just inevitable, but desirable. In his first interview after securing a City job, Nathan explained that the top quartile of graduate trainees in terms of performance at his US investment bank was paid significant bonuses of up to 100 per cent of their salary at the end of the year, while those in the bottom quartile were summarily dismissed. He was ranked top among his peers and got 80–90 per cent of his salary as a bonus, reaching an annual salary of nearly £100,000.

Nathan bought into the work culture of the financial world, knowing that working hours in the City were extremely demanding and that anyone who suspected otherwise and came into it "hadn't done their research". He suggested that it was "part of the job" and "what we signed up for", but that "in the long run, it pays off". At the same time, it was all-consuming. He described his time in the US as "working fairly hard but partying harder", a situation reversed when he returned to London, where he found the hours "brutal": "There was a stretch in January through to about March where it was just non-stop, like ... weekends every other week. ... I did 127 hours in one week". There was very little time for "playing hard" because the hours he was required to work were so demanding and the pressure was immense. Nathan spoke of his employer "buying" his "youth" and felt that he was "selling" his "soul" to advance the organization he was working for. He knew the required working hours would not improve significantly for a number of years and that "the question then becomes: 'Are you prepared to wait or sacrifice six years to reach a stage where you can have a life?'" (Interview 7).

For Nathan, these doubts grew, and he felt frustrated that progression rates were effectively limited by company policy – staff only became eligible for promotion every three years, even if the compensation for that came in the form of a possible large annual bonus. He also began to feel that money alone was not enough – he was professionally ambitious and wanted more responsibility. He moved to a different post within the same firm to enhance his longer-term career opportunities, rather than for short-term financial gain: "I'd rather have zero bonus and progress in my career and get promoted more quickly and get more responsibility" (Interview 8). Even so, aged just 23, Nathan's salary in his new post was £60,000, plus the chance of a bonus of up to 100 per cent of that. He said that he was headhunted daily by private equity firms and hedge funds but chose to remain in his existing post for a little longer while, at the same time, starting to get involved in the start-up scene in order to begin his own business, which was his original long-term plan. He was ready to take risks to achieve his future career goals, unencumbered by other commitments. As he explained:

> 'You know, now is the time to take some risks in life, when you're young and you can still recover. If you go and try and do something when you're 22 or 23 and it fails, fine, come back, work in the City again or you get another job, fine. But if you get married and have kids and have a mortgage and you've bought a house, you can't all of a sudden drop it all and go and quit and start your own firm, or change job, it becomes a lot more difficult.' (Interview 8)

By 2016, Nathan had left his role in the City bank and started work with a new firm as an investment executive after being approached by a firm of headhunters. Seeking to minimize risk, Nathan had done his due-diligence checks on the firm, taking a day's leave and, in his own words, "staking out" their offices to see what time people came and went for work in order to see whether the sales pitch from the recruitment agency matched the reality, and he felt it did. Nathan was now working 40–50 hours a week; the pay was similar to his last role (£60,000 plus a potentially sizeable bonus), but the hours were much better, and he could enjoy 'downtime' in the evenings and weekends that he had not been able to previously.

However, Nathan was already thinking of his next move, planning to set up a firm to advise investors and other City professionals in another year or so with one of his flatmates, a student friend with whom he had lived since moving to London. He acknowledged that this represented a risk, but he was confident he would be able to find another City role if things did not work out, having a strong track record of working in the City since graduating four years previously. He also had economic resources he could utilize, having saved money while working at his previous firm by leading a relatively frugal lifestyle. Champagne and sharp suits were of no interest to Nathan; rather, he talked of "going back to a student [lifestyle] of pasta and toast" (Interview 9). The security of having economic capital behind him, as well as the social networks he had established, meant that Nathan had complete confidence in himself to try and achieve his long-term ambitions:

> 'The question is in the longer term, do you back yourself to get the job that you want, and I do. So, if it means I have to take a step down in terms of level or in terms of job … then that's worth it because I have given it a shot and it hasn't worked out, which is completely fine, but that's the risk you've got to take. … It's more the sense of, I think, just being a little bit, probably, impatient and overambitious. But if you don't try these things, then they never happen and you find out that before too long, I'm in my mid-30s with a wife and child and a mortgage, and I can't do that anymore, and I think, well, I will spend the rest of my days thinking "What if? What if? What if it might have all worked and I might have started a successful company?"'(Interview 9)

By 2017, four years after graduation, Nathan had made the move to set up his own company with his friend from university. Nathan compared running his own business to "like being in exam season at university: you're always working, you don't switch off really ever, but you just have different periods of intensity" (Interview 10). He seemed to be relishing the situation and found not having to please or appease managers very satisfying:

'So, it's not always like very, very intense, and it's not like someone else is telling you what you need to do; it's just completely self-imposed pressure. If I decide that I don't want to work tomorrow, I don't have to work tomorrow. But then I look at my bank balance and I see that it's going like this and that the company needs to be successful, so I need to come back and do a bit more work.' (Interview 10)

When asked how he imagined the future four years after graduation, he said:

'Hopefully, I will still be doing something I love, whether that is because I'm still running the company and it's grown and we're in the US or we're in Asia, and I'm working with great people that I enjoy working with, or it's not that and I've managed to find my way back to another finance job.' (Interview 10)

Harvey: working his way back into the middle class

Whereas Nathan was able to consolidate the advantages of his established middle-class background, giving him immense confidence in his capacity to succeed and epitomizing the 21st-century 'top boy', who is endowed with knowledge and intellectual authority, and who excels on all levels, Harvey was inspired by a determination to work his way back into the middle class. His vision of the future combined working-class notions of masculinity focused on physicality, linked to the need to be a provider and a protector of others, with a belief that he could excel academically and therefore move himself and his family back into the middle class.

Before Harvey was born, his mother had established a career as an exchange dealer in the City but was made redundant after she came back from maternity leave. She then had a period of unemployment and claimed benefits before finding a job as a telephone operator, raising her two children on her own. Harvey regarded their position now as working class, following their experience of downward mobility. Perhaps in response to this, he was especially driven by financial success. He certainly aspired to the 'top boy' lifestyle of popular discourse. He wanted to 'get to the top' quickly, earn the big money available in the finance world and enjoy a flamboyant, hedonistic lifestyle, replete with glamour and conspicuous consumption. At the same time, his aspiration to be a 'top boy' was also driven by a determination to assume responsibility for providing for his mother and sister.

The family lived in an Essex town close to the border with east London, which gave him a degree of proximity to, as well as familiarity with, the career and the lifestyle he aspired to. The route to a job in the City, which he suggested "reeked of masculinity" (Interview 6), was one quite often taken by people from that part of the country, especially following the expansion of London's financial services sector in the aftermath of the Big Bang. Geographical proximity of his family home, to which he could return after university, and a reasonable familiarity with its cultural milieu (see also Chapter 3) gave Harvey a significant head start in seeking a career in the finance sector in the City.

A City career was not Harvey's first choice. When he started university, he talked of a "passion for fashion" and would ideally have pursued this as a career. He explained that his family circumstances pushed him to choose finance: "If I was from a wealthier background, I would definitely have picked … the priority would be on what's going to be fulfilling, rather than what's going to earn me money" (Interview 1). He progressed to the UoB to study economics, assuming that studying this subject, which he did not especially enjoy, was the best way to secure a career in finance.

During his time at university, Harvey demonstrated significant entrepreneurial flair and willingness to take financial risks. He was known as someone who could get hold of things for people and could turn his hand readily to making a profit. He had worked part-time as a market trader before starting university, and as a student, he had made money by travelling to France, buying wine in a French supermarket, bringing it back to Bristol and selling it on at a profit to some of his wealthier peers. He even bought and adapted a van especially, strengthening its suspension to enable him to trade with a greater volume of wine. Harvey had been given the nickname 'Del-Boy' by some of his friends, after the character in the TV programme 'Only Fools and Horses', and he enjoyed performing the 'loveable rogue' character.

Harvey was extremely confident in his abilities and his capacity to use his personal charm, a form of embodied cultural capital that he was fully prepared to mobilize for maximum benefit. He felt that he would excel in an interview or similar situation where his 'natural' charisma could come to the fore. However, he was relatively ignorant of the 'rules of the game' (Bathmaker et al, 2013) as far as securing a position in the City was concerned. For example, he was unaware of the de facto requirement to get an internship with a City firm while at university, as many of his peers had managed to do. However, he did realize that studying at a prestigious university would confer an advantage over others who had not done so. As he suggested part-way into his studies: "When it comes to university, where you went is a lot more important than what you did" (Interview 4). However, it was only part-way through his undergraduate studies that Harvey became aware that his economics degree would not be enough in itself and that he needed to get an internship to be able to compete for the most competitive graduate opportunities in the City. After his last exams, he managed to secure an internship through a chance meeting with someone who was able to offer him a two-month opportunity in London. This was followed by another in India, and he was able to obtain, first, a position as a broker in a high-profile City firm and then, soon after, another as a trader in a second company. As Harvey had said previously, he was eager for success and prepared to change roles or move firms to achieve it more quickly.

While Harvey had lacked the knowledge regarding the 'rules of the game' when initially considering a career in the City, he learnt them quickly and became very good at playing. As a high-level sportsman, his 'natural' desire to compete came to the fore in an environment where it was highly valued. He relished the competitive aspects of the work and associated lifestyle, and embraced the evaluation of financial risk that the job entailed. His approach demonstrates an aspiration to be an archetypal 21st-century 'top boy'; that is, to utilize his masculinity to garner advantage in work and leisure, and to strive to have it all.

Harvey's working life was stressful and physically demanding. He started at 6.30 am and would work until quite late before going out with clients or friends afterwards most nights, rarely getting home before midnight and "only sleeping four or five hours" (Interview

7). Socializing with clients after work was an expectation of the role, but it was something he enjoyed and excelled at. However, having such busy and tiring evenings during the week did not prevent Harvey from 'playing hard' with friends at weekends and in holiday periods, including playing sports, drinking, partying and going away on frequent trips in the UK and abroad. He told of one such trip during his first year after graduation that involved a golf weekend in the north of England, immediately followed by six nights in Ibiza and then a road trip through five different European countries for another week.

Yet, in early 2016, 18 months following his first interview after graduation, Harvey had changed his life dramatically. He had left the City of London and was living in Australia. We learned that Harvey had switched roles and firms several times in the City before leaving the UK, as things had not been happening for him as quickly as he had hoped in terms of career advancement. He said that he had been experiencing "itchy feet" and so began looking for exciting new challenges, and he decided to try and find work in Australia's financial sector as a new "adventure" (Interview 9). A recruitment company found him such a role, but he decided to take some time off to travel the country before starting work and to visit some friends he had there.

Despite his initial intentions to continue working in finance in Australia, an alternative career pathway soon loomed into view, one that resonated with things he had done as a student in Bristol:

> 'I was having a holiday … and then we went to some really nice wineries in Queensland, and I basically, sort of, fell in love with this winery place. … So, I just decided to ditch [finance] altogether, and I've actually been contracted as a winemaker for the last three … four months.' (Interview 9)

At this point in time, Harvey was enjoying his life as a winemaker in Australia tremendously, and it was, in a sense, a revisiting of the entrepreneurial 'wine-importing' activities that he had been involved in as a student. Significant symbolic capital is attached to wine as a product, and it has obvious links to the conspicuous consumption and hedonism that Harvey enjoys. He had the self-confidence to believe that he would be successful at winemaking should he commit fully to it, though at that stage, he was not ruling out a return to the UK and to working back in the City again one day. He had been careful to maintain his networks there and was confident that his skills, charisma and contacts would mean that he could return if he wanted to, even if the jobs he had done there had not been quite as enjoyable or satisfying as he had anticipated while at university: "The banking industry is not quite as good as I think it was. … [It's] a little bit more regulated now, so it's not quite as fun as I think some of the guys who were over there ten years ago would probably tell me" (Interview 9). He talked about perhaps having been too single-minded, too serious in terms of his work and related lifestyle aspirations, when in London, compared to his time making wine in Australia:

> 'Yeah, I was serious then. I think I just switch it on and off really. I probably will go back to being serious at some point because it is a huge change of pace. At the moment, I'm just so content, but I think eventually, I'll probably get itchy feet because I've got … it's such a juxtaposition from, like, the really long weeks and fast pace: a lot of pressure to no stress whatsoever.' (Interview 9)

We can see here the negative impact of the 'top boys' imperative, which requires a commitment to working and playing with intensity. Harvey's detour into winemaking is, in many ways, a reaction to the unsustainable demands of having it all. By the summer of 2017, Harvey had returned to the UK and was working for a specialist recruitment company that focused on the City. He had made the shift in roles as a consequence of having worked with the company when looking to return to London from Australia. Having spoken to a recruiter at length to research the options open to him, Harvey decided that their job seemed more interesting and was potentially as lucrative as the roles he had left before leaving for Australia: "I [was] more impressed with the headhunter that I was using … than some of the banks I was working with." As Harvey explained: "I was hoping that the people I [now work] for were going to find me the job I wanted, or the job that I planned to get … [but]

I ended up working for them as opposed to taking one of the jobs that they supply" (Interview 10). Leveraging his knowledge of the sector, his charm and his social capital from professional networks, Harvey suggested that his change in career direction was "quite an easy transition to make" (Interview 10). He was employing his fine-honed entrepreneurial and social skills developed through his time at university and subsequent careers in the City and wine industry, and said: "I think ... we're effectively just selling something. It's just people rather than a commodity, I suppose, or a product" (Interview 10).

Another appeal of his recruitment post was that he had greater autonomy over his conditions of work. He effectively kept his own hours and did not have a direct manager to whom he was accountable. If he worked hard and was successful, he got very well paid, which had always been important to him; he felt he deserved that financial recognition and reward. Harvey referred to recruitment as a "sink or swim" (Interview 10) environment, which very much appealed to his competitive approach to life. It was also potentially very well rewarded; Harvey said that he was on target to earn about £120,000 for the year, certainly enough for the 'top boy' lifestyle he desired, particularly given that he was able to live back with his mother, keeping his overheads manageable while saving to buy his own place. His desire for 'top boy' status was embedded in his vision of himself as the male breadwinner and his claim to a masculine ideal of head of household.

While Harvey's narrative demonstrates similar levels of successful high-status career making as seen in the progress of Nathan's career, rather than consolidating a middle-class position, Harvey's trajectory and outcome are, in many ways, a response to his family's downward mobility, which fuelled his determination to secure a better class position through financial security. He was able to use his 'London capital' – a combination of his family's geographical location in London and London 'cool' and confidence (see Chapter 3) – along with the cultural capital he built through his time at university and on-the-job social capital, to position himself as a key player in his industry of choice, displaying a resourcefulness in capital conversion and an astute capacity for learning and adapting to the Bourdieusian 'game'. This stands in contrast to Leo's experience of struggling with the rules of the game and the conditions of working in the finance industry outside of the City of London.

Leo: a career in finance as a route to security

Leo came from a working-class family. His father was a train driver and his mother was not employed outside the home, and he grew up in an economically deprived area of south Wales. In his first interview, Leo described his ideal future as an aeronautical engineer. However, he was unable to pursue this goal because he needed a maths A-Level to get a place on an engineering degree and he had dropped maths at the age of 16. No one had advised him of this at the time, and he could not subsequently envisage postponing university for two years in order to study for a maths A-Level.

He progressed to UWE to study economics and finance but was ambivalent about a career in this area, not least after working in an accountant's office during a gap year before university, which he described as "dull" (Interview 1). Even though he recognized that this work experience was very useful in terms of his CV, he struggled from the very beginning to see a future in accounting:

Interviewer: Have you got a career in mind?
Leo: Not really no, it's quite daunting. But I didn't enjoy accounting all that much, so I don't really want to go back to that route. (Interview 1)

Throughout his studies, Leo achieved high grades, culminating in a first-class honours degree. However, while he was very successful in his academic studies, unlike Nathan and Harvey, he did not invest in building his professional profile and cultivating additional capital. He joined the climbing society towards the end of his second year but was not involved in any other extra-curricular activities, and he had no time to take on an internship, as he worked in bars and supermarkets during term time and his summer vacation.

He seemed at a loss regarding his future career direction, and it was striking in what he told us that he appeared to be very much left to work out a future for himself when what he needed was direction and support. He did not have a sense of how he might use such opportunities as the Milk Round (where employers visit universities as part of their attraction and recruitment process): "Milk Round? No. I went to the one careers fair when it was in the University Exhibition and Conference Centre, but I didn't stay there very long, I didn't think I got much from it." Even towards the end of his studies, Leo was struggling to make himself put in applications for jobs and graduate schemes: "Another thing that I was meant to do is apply for grad jobs. I've only applied for two and got turned down for one, still waiting on the other one, but, yeah, I haven't really put as much effort into finding a graduate scheme as I should have" (Interview 6). He had no family networks to fall back on, as he explains in the following:

Interviewer: And in terms of your parents and stuff, you know, with their, sort of, jobs and things, are there any links that they could ...? I know your dad works on the railways.

Leo: I'm not sure how their recruitment system works. I don't think, yeah, I don't think, it's all done from like central offices, so it's not. ...

Interviewer: So, it's not, like, 'Here's my lad, he wants a job.'

Leo: Yeah, it used to be like that, but no. (Interview 6)

Despite graduating with a first-class degree, Leo's progression to graduate employment did not follow a linear and smooth trajectory. Over the summer after graduation, he was offered the opportunity to attend the assessment centre for one of the 'Big Four' accounting firms. However, he was unsuccessful and "out of desperation" (Interview 7), he turned to casual unskilled work (first as a delivery driver for six months and then in a post-room for another six months). He was not in a position to take time out to think through a route to a desired career, with no one who could support him to do this, and he struggled with knowing how to go about moving forward:

Interviewer: So, this sounds quite clinical now, but have you got a strategy for where you want to go next?

Leo: No, not at all. (Interview 7)

He eventually quit his job in the post-room and started applying for jobs in accounting, but after "a few dozen" (Interview 9) unsuccessful applications, he was under pressure to find a job, as he had spent all his savings. At this point, he managed to get a fixed-term contract in a university research grants office. This invigorated Leo's interest in the sector, and what was significant for his future was that this post gave him a career pathway to follow. He began to envisage a future career in a finance department of a university – it appeared viable and offered a structured career route: "Somewhere like where I'm working now would be good … because you could, like, work up, there's, like, loads of opportunities in the university. In the finance department alone, there's, like, 160 people or something" (Interview 9). At the end of his fixed-term contract, Leo was offered a permanent post, and he started applying internally for higher positions in the finance department of the university. Although he did not feel "particularly driven" towards his career and still felt that career planning "always seems like something for further in the future" (Interview 9), this secure post, with structured opportunities for progression, provided the conditions that enabled him to imagine and realize a career future.

Of central importance to Leo was financial stability and avoiding risk and precarity. As he explained: "I just want to get … somewhere permanent and settled. Once I know that I'm going to have a job permanently, I think then I'll be able to look forward" (Interview 10). His social life was not about a 'champagne and sharp suits' lifestyle or the conspicuous consumption sought by Harvey. Leo liked outdoor living, notably climbing, and occasionally going drinking with friends and housemates. He enjoyed travel and hoped to go through Europe and/or the US in a campervan one day, and he talked of having longer-term ambitions to move to Canada or New Zealand.

He said he was very happy in his job, and despite starting to find it a bit repetitive, he had not started looking for other roles. He often repeated the sentiment that "there's much more to life than work" and enjoyed having a work–life balance that allowed him to spend time on outdoor pursuits, such as cycling and climbing. Establishing a longer-term graduate life in Bristol was part of this:

'I'm happy, and I've got a stable relationship going, girlfriend, that's always good. But, yeah, moving back to Bristol was the big one for me because I wasn't particularly happy when I was back in [hometown]; it was fine, but I much prefer being here, and I'm glad that I have moved here. I can see me being here for a long time.' (Interview 10)

Reflecting on the progress of his career in the four years following graduation, he suggested that he had not really progressed far, as:

'I haven't been that career driven over the last couple of years; I've just been complacent in my job, so I haven't given it that much thought really. But, yeah, I don't feel I've gone particularly well on my career, and I don't feel I am particularly stretched at the minute.' (Interview 10)

In terms of future career plans, Leo suggested that:

'I won't give my career itself that much thought; I just, sort of, take it as it comes. Because I haven't spent a great deal of time looking at other jobs or opportunities where I am now, I tend to focus more on stuff outside of work. Like, when I'm outside the working day, I spend more time just focusing on other stuff, rather than thinking about my career, because I don't feel particularly driven towards my career. I'm happy just getting by for now and just keep … that always seems like something for further in the future. … I just aspire to be, like, comfortable with what I do and happy with what I do, and so long as I've got enough money just to be comfortable and happy, that's fine.' (Interview 10)

Unlike Nathan and Harvey, Leo does not live up to the demands of the 'top boys' discourse and pushes back against its expectations. He seeks financial stability and wishes to avoid risk, rather than aiming to gain recognition through forms of hegemonic masculinity based in sporting prowess and excelling academically and in a career. On the one hand, this could be read as making the choice of the necessary; he turns away from the choice that he is effectively denied (Bourdieu, 1984). On the other, his narrative could be seen to suggest the possibility of alternative values that go against the demands of 21st-century forms of hegemonic masculinity, as well as dominant expectations of what it means to be a successful graduate.

Conclusion

This chapter has highlighted key class-based differences among young men with aspirations to have careers in finance. Both Nathan and Harvey, in different ways, epitomize approaches to securing status as 'top boys': Nathan through business success and Harvey through financial success and adopting the role of the male breadwinner. They both had different opportunities open to them for inhabiting this identity, and these are embedded in the habitus of their original class positionings. As part of the established middle class, Nathan had active social connections and hot knowledge (Ball and Vincent, 1998), which facilitated access to high-level employment, as well as his orientation to the 'risk' of starting his own business. Harvey, epitomizing the fallen middle class, sought to return his family to a secure middle-class position. He had strong awareness and 'street knowledge' of what was involved in being part of that world, but no active connections and no hot knowledge to make it happen. Consequently, he learned as he went along and began to understand the requirements of the game and the forms of capital that he needed to build. In both cases, we can see repackaged hegemonic masculinity (Ingram and Waller 2014) through both young men's strategies for success and dominance, as well as quest for self-sufficiency and actualization; in Harvey's case, we also see this through the assumption of the role of male breadwinner.

Leo, from a working-class background, stands in contrast to them both. He stays and seeks work in Bristol, rather than moving to the City, and is not committed to the pull of the 'top boy' discourse of success. Moreover, while he aspires to a career in finance, he is limited in his opportunities to achieve a high-status career in this field, having neither the hot knowledge nor the social connections to forge a highly lucrative career, nor the desire to have a life dominated by work. Instead, over time, he works out a career route that enables him to progress and succeed on his own terms, and to find fulfilment in his world beyond work. Comparing the narratives of these three young men highlights how, particularly in such industries as finance, the making of contemporary masculinities through a 'top boys' discourse promotes an understanding of success as involving competition, risk taking and the valorization of financial reward. While Leo is able to realize a meaningful future, in the shadow of a 'top boys' discourse he has not matched expectations. Moreover, narrow definitions of success encouraged by the promotion of high-achieving, high-earning career routes in higher education policy reinforce this discourse and foster a strategic and instrumental approach to graduate labour market transitions. In this chapter, we have shown how this allows particular forms of masculinity to flourish and middle-class privilege to prevail.

References

Anderson, E. (2009) *Inclusive Masculinity: The Changing Nature of Masculinities*, New York: Routledge.

Ball, S.J. and Vincent, C. (1998) 'I heard it on the grapevine': 'hot' knowledge and school choice, *British Journal of Sociology of Education*, 19(3): 377–400.

Bathmaker, A.M., Ingram, N. and Waller, R. (2013) Higher education, social class and the mobilisation of capitals: recognising and playing the game, *British Journal of Sociology of Education*, 34(5/6): 723–43.

Bourdieu, P. (1984) *Distinction: A Social Critique of the Judgement of Taste*, London: Routledge & Kegan and Paul Ltd.

Bourdieu, P. (1986) The forms of capital, in J. Richardson (ed) *Handbook of Theory and Research in Education*, Westport, CT: Greenwood, pp 241–58.

Bourdieu, P. (1990) *The Logic of Practice*, Stanford, CA: Stanford University Press.

Bowers-Brown, T., Ingram, N. and Burke, C. (2019) Higher education and aspiration, *International Studies in Sociology of Education*, 28(3–4): 207–14.

Brown, P. and Tannock, S. (2009) Education, meritocracy and the global war for talent, *Journal of Education Policy*, 24(4): 377–92.

Brown, P., Lauder, H. and Ashton, D. (2011) *The Global Auction, the Broken Promises of Education, Jobs and Incomes*, Oxford: Oxford University Press.

Brown, P., Lauder, H. and Cheung, S.Y. (2020) *Death of Human Capital? Its Failed Promise and How to Renew It in an Age of Disruption*, Oxford: Oxford University Press.

Connell, R.W. (1995) *Masculinities*, Cambridge: Polity.

Connell, R.W. (2000) *The Men and the Boys*, Cambridge: Polity.

Connell, R.W. and Messerschmidt, J.W. (2005) Hegemonic masculinity: rethinking the concept, *Gender & Society*, 19(6): 829–59.

Harris, A. (2004) *Future Girl: Young Women in the Twenty-First Century*, London: Routledge.

Ingram, N. and Waller, R. (2014) Degrees of masculinity: working and middle class male undergraduates' constructions of contemporary masculine identities, in S. Roberts (ed) *Debating Modern Masculinities: Change, Continuity, Crisis?*, Basingstoke: Palgrave MacMillan, pp 35–51.

Ingram, N. and Waller, R. (2015) Higher education and the reproduction of social elites, *Discover Society*, 20, https://archive. discoversociety.org/2015/05/05/higher-education-and-the-reproduction-of-social-elites/

Longlands, H. (2020) *Gender, Space and City Bankers*, Abingdon: Routledge.

McCormack, M. (2014) The intersection of youth masculinities, decreasing homophobia and class: an ethnography, *The British Journal of Sociology*, 65(1): 130–49.

McDowell, L. (2011) *Capital Culture: Gender at Work in the City*, Oxford: Blackwell.

McRobbie, A. (2007) 'Top girls?', *Cultural Studies*, 21(4–5): 718–37.

McRobbie, A. (2009) *The Aftermath of Feminism: Gender, Culture and Social Change*, London: Sage.

Metcalfe, H. and Rolfe, H. (2009) *Employment and Earnings in the Finance Sector: A Gender Analysis*, Research Report 17, London and Manchester: Equality and Human Rights Commission.

STEM Women (2021) Home page, www.stemwomen.com

Wakeling, P. and Savage, M. (2015) Entry to elite positions and the stratification of higher education in Britain, *The Sociological Review*, 63(2): 290–320.

7

Following Dreams and Temporary Escapes: The Impacts of Cruel Optimism

Introduction

> 'I'm going to get this really amazing job, and I'm going
> to change the world, and I'm going to be middle class,
> then I'll have, like, a great amount of money coming
> in, and I'll have a nice suburban house and drive a jeep.'
> (Interview 6)

This was how Jasmine, a white, working-class sociology graduate
from UWE, described her idyllic dreams of what her life after
university would be like. This upbeat dream of the future is typical
of many of the participants in the Paired Peers study. As young
people make their early steps into working lives, going to university
is seen to offer a passport to worldly success and a secure future
in a decently rewarded job, and is reflected in their optimism.
Indeed, as we have discussed in Chapter 1, university participation
is constructed in policy and political discourse as the ticket to
the good life and a route to social mobility (Ingram and Gamsu,
2022). The pervasive discourse of social mobility within the higher
education policy domain has promoted and maintained a belief
in the employment rewards of higher education, which, in turn,
has encouraged working-class young people's participation. This
prospect is particularly alluring to those, like Jasmine, who are the

first in their family to enter higher education, who understandably bank on education as the route to a more prosperous future. For many middle-class young people, who see going to university as the taken-for-granted thing to do (see Bathmaker et al, 2016), the prospect may not evoke in them the same kind of optimistic visions of class mobility; rather, it brings tacit expectations of consolidating their class position and contributing to continuing class reproduction. Yet, most students entering higher education will have their own aspirations and their own visions of success, which, as the chapters in this book show, are more diverse than narrow measures based on employment destination and earnings. In this chapter, we consider the motivations and dreams of participants in the Paired Peers study, and look at how what actually awaits lives up to these dreams through the eyes of two graduates: Jasmine and Martin. We utilize the concept of 'cruel optimism' (Berlant, 2006, 2019) to consider the heartbreak of broken dreams. Berlant (2019) describes cruel optimism as 'heartbreak that the world isn't worthy of our attachment to it, that it gives us objects or ways of life or forms of life that are constantly betraying us'. In this chapter, we show how university participation can operate as a form of cruel optimism for the working class, while maintaining optimistic possibilities for the middle class.

Aspirations of the 'degree generation'

The book from Phase 1 of the Paired Peers project, which recruited 90 students from the two universities in Bristol, the UoB and UWE, and followed them through three years of undergraduate study, bore the subtitle *The Degree Generation* (Bathmaker et al, 2016). We have adopted this as the main title for the follow-up book because so many young people of this (the millennial) generation see university as an expected or hoped-for life stage and a necessary step on the journey to adulthood. This has long been true for middle-class school leavers, but in recent decades, as participation has increased and routine and semi-routine occupations in the labour market have contracted (Goldthorpe, 2016), many working-class families have also developed aspirations for their children to go to university (Atkinson and Bradley, 2013; Bathmaker et al, 2016; Harrison and Waller, 2018). For working-class families, however, there is not often the insistent pressure to go to university exerted by middle-class families (Walkerdine et al, 2001), where university becomes a necessary and required step, rather than a possibility. The following comment from Jade, a working-class graduate from Bristol, is indicative of this phenomenon:

> 'My mum and dad always, kind of, like, promoted, "Yeah, uni is a good thing", but if I said to them, "I don't want to go", they would understand, I think. My dad always said, "Do what makes you feel happy", but they still, like, tried to push it a little bit, not, like, pressurize, but just to say, "It's a good thing". Because they didn't go to uni, my mum and dad didn't go, so I suppose you always want the best for your children.' (Interview 1)

As noted in Chapter 1, this normalization of higher education has been fostered by social mobility discourses in both the political and the policy arenas (Milburn, 2009, 2012a, 2012b; Waller et al, 2014; Ingram and Gamsu, 2022), leading to an appetite for increasing university access and participation from 35 per cent to over 50 per cent in the last 20 years (DfES, 1991; Public Accounts Committee, 2009; Boliver, 2011). However, at the same time, the supply of graduate-level jobs has been decreasing. Goldthorpe (2016) shows that between 1951 and 2011, there has been a significant expansion of professional occupations; however, the growth of this section of the labour market has slowed down considerably, resulting in diminishing financial returns to higher education investment. Similarly, a series of studies by Philip Brown and colleagues (Brown, 1999, 2003; Brown et al, 2011, 2020) has shown that there is less room at the top and that young people have been caught in an 'opportunity trap', whereby they have invested time and energy in attending university only to find on graduation that they have to return to non-graduate work, as we will see in the case of Jasmine in this chapter. Her story is one of 'cruel optimism' (Berlant, 2011), whereby her initial dreams of success, security and prosperity were thwarted by the reality of the structure of a graduate labour market that can no longer deliver the promised opportunities.

In this chapter, we bring the notion of cruel optimism into conversation with Bourdieu's (1986) account of capital to explore the ways in which high aspirations and dreams are a key component of the functioning of neoliberalism, allowing for the development of forms of capital that ultimately do not automatically realize their value, particularly for some people from working-class backgrounds in contemporary graduate labour markets. We go beyond a consideration of stocks of capital to focus on the capital conversion process as a crucial site for exploring the realization of dreams and aspirations. This affords the opportunity to expose the social processes at play in recognizing and misrecognizing the capitals of differently positioned young people on the graduate labour market, and to examine what is ultimately converted and symbolically legitimated.

As our study, among others, shows, working-class young people are disadvantaged when it comes to gaining a graduate job (Reay, 2017; Friedman and Laurison, 2020). The nationwide Futuretrack study of graduates found that only a minority accessed traditional 'graduate jobs', such as medicine, law and accountancy (Purcell et al, 2013), while a Social Mobility Commission (2019) analysis of the Labour Force Survey shows that 60 per cent of people from a professional/managerial background are employed in professional/managerial jobs, whereas only 34 per cent of people from working-class backgrounds are employed in the professional/managerial occupational group. In addition, those from disadvantaged backgrounds are more likely to attend post-92 universities, which can limit their chances of getting such jobs due to the hierarchically stratified nature of the UK higher education system and employers' (mis)recognition of degrees from different institutions. As Ingram and Allen (2019) show, graduate employers attach more value to graduates from elite institutions than newer universities, even though the sector is regulated through the Quality Assurance Agency, which, in theory, assures parity of degree outcomes across all higher education institutions.

Given this wider picture, it is interesting to consider the expectations of students in the Paired Peers cohort as they started on their academic journeys. We asked all the students what motivated them to go to university. A common answer was to get a good job or 'a better life', though others talked of wanting to study a particular discipline that they had enjoyed at school. Regardless of social class, for some, it was part of a plan to achieve a future career that they had wanted for many years – as a lawyer, a teacher, an engineer and so on – while for others, it was simply to have a career that they were (at that stage) unable to plan, define or envisage (for more on unplanned graduate pathways, see Chapter 8).

The majority of the participants had no clearly formulated career plans or aspirations at the start of their degrees. This appears to contrast with the findings of Brooks and Everett (2008), whose study of graduates from a range of institutions noted that the majority did engage in life planning. However, some of the planning evolved at a much later stage than the start of the degree, which accords with our findings; moreover, they found that the more privileged students were less likely to have life plans, and that too was evident among our participants. Those who did have ideas mentioned banking, teaching, engineering, policing, charity work, barrister, solicitor, international development, forensic psychology, air traffic control, animal conservation, acting, writing and music. Some of the more politically orientated social science participants talked about not being exactly sure about their aspirations, but knowing that they wanted an 'ethical career', and others talked about giving something back to society. Both Jasmine and Martin, who we discuss in the following, are examples of young people with a social conscience who want to not only make a life, but also make a difference. We present the narratives of these two graduates in this chapter because they stand in stark contrast to one another and epitomize the difference that class background can make to employment outcomes and opportunities; realizing dreams is a class issue.

Jasmine's story: cruel optimism and broken dreams

We started this chapter with an excerpt from an early interview where Jasmine, a working-class sociology student at UWE, joked about her dream middle-class life. In reality, Jasmine aspired to find work that she found meaningful, rather than a life of luxury, but she assumed that as a graduate, work and a decent standard of living would evolve together.

Jasmine was the first in her family to go to university. Her father, whom she described as "the cleverest person I know", had been to further education college but dropped out and became a self-employed sound engineer: "He recorded bands in a tiny little shack in our garden" (Interview 1). Subsequently, he bought a cheap house and did it up as a holiday let in south Cornwall, where the family lived. Jasmine described her mother as a housewife, but she also assisted her husband in his ventures. For example, when he worked as a music teacher to get money to do up the houses, her mother framed photographs of the music students to sell them for extra funds. Her parents were creative and resourceful, and they were supportive of Jasmine's educational ambitions.

Jasmine went to what she designated "the worst school in Cornwall" full of "disruptive kids" (Interview 1), but she did well academically, and her passion for sociology took her to study the subject at UWE. She arrived full of excitement and desire to do well. Unusually for a working-class undergraduate, she did not work during term time, following her father's advice that it would be detrimental to her studies. This led her into considerable financial difficulties, so she had to borrow from her parents, and in the summer vacations, she took jobs in bakeries in Cornwall. Academically, she did well; in each year, she had a mix of 2:1 and first-class grades, and she ended with a high upper second (68 per cent).

She had always been a little uncertain about what she would do for a career, telling us in the first two years of undergraduate study that she had thoughts of social work or charity work, something helping young people:

'So, I've always had at the back of my mind that I maybe wanted to be a social worker, although there would be a lot of emotional pressure with that. One of my best friend's mum is a really high-up social worker down in Cornwall, and she comes home pretty much every day crying for a good hour, just has to have a glass of wine to settle her nerves, you know, I don't know if I could cope with that. … I was thinking of going along the lines of maybe being a counsellor for mental health patients. Yeah, that would be good because I like to

listen to people and I like to try and give them advice. …
I think they're my main two.' (Interview 3)

In her final year, she appeared to become clearer about the future. She wanted to move to Manchester, where her new boyfriend lived, and to pursue a master's degree in social work, though she had not acquired the work experience that was needed to qualify for such a course. However, there was a conflict here with another desire that had been a running theme in her interviews: "I really, really want to go travelling with my boyfriend. We're really ambitious to, like, travel the world together. I want to save up on my year off, well, sort of save up for a bit, do a bit of travelling" (Interview 5). Having put off the idea of a master's on the grounds that she needed a break from study, and in any case not having the necessary work experience to be offered a place, Jasmine struggled to find a job after her move to Manchester. She told us that she had applied for 40 to 50 jobs, which was not untypical for the less privileged graduates in the Paired Peers study. Eventually, she gained a job as a low-paid care worker with the elderly. While this was not a very pleasant experience – she explained that "It was just so intense, it was serious shift work, it was split shifts, I just couldn't be doing with that, couldn't do it" (Interview 7) – it was useful because it helped her secure a job with a charity as a mental health support worker dealing with convicted women. She enthused about this work:

'I love making a difference to people's lives. … There's so many things I love about it; I just love it. I love the responsibility as well; I've got quite a lot of responsibility. Yeah, just making a difference really. It's really scary at times, and it's really boring at times, and it's really sad at times, and it's just everything. Every day's different; that's what I like about it the most.' (Interview 7)

The charity offered her training and supported her to complete a National Vocational Qualification (NVQ) Level 3[1] in mental

---

[1] In the UK, NVQs are work-based awards involving training and assessment. The Level 3 awards are equivalent to A-Levels, which

health and social care, leading to a promotion to a more senior role as team leader. However, just as she seemed to be developing a career trajectory, there were setbacks: difficult experiences at work, assault by a client and a lack of support and advice from managers. As she stated: "We're underpaid, understaffed, overworked, and we're getting loads of verbal abuse off the women. And no consequences put in place, no support with the staff. I'm literally there for my NVQ and I'm out of there" (Interview 9). Experiencing stress and anxiety led her to hand in her resignation. It seemed as if Jasmine's life was falling apart. She was missing Bristol and student life, struggling financially on her salary of £17,000 a year and having counselling. It was then that she made the dramatic decision to return to live with her parents in Cornwall despite knowing that employment prospects there were poor. Her final interview with the Paired Peers project was painful to listen to:

> 'I was living in Manchester in March 2014, decided to move home, jack all of my life in and start again. So, I did, and here I am now: unemployed, living at home feeling like I'm 16 again. So, it's very strange. I hated my job and things weren't particularly amazing with my then boyfriend. I wanted more; I wanted to get home. So, I just came home. I just thought, "Oh, bugger it, I'll just go." So, I did. I just took the plunge, like, jacked all of my life in and started again.' (Interview 10)

Jasmine's story illustrates the struggles many less privileged young adults are going through. Jasmine found the experience of being unemployed and having to sign on humiliating and depressing:

> 'Oh, it's horrendous … you have to have 100 per cent commitment to job searching. … It was like 30-odd hours a week searching for jobs. And, obviously, it's only

_____

are pre-Bachelor-level qualifications that can be used for entry to undergraduate study.

Cornwall, so there aren't 30-odd hours' worth of jobs to look through. … I had to write like a work-search diary and then had to go in each week for a meeting so that I would meet the Universal Credit requirement.' (Interview 10)

For somebody already suffering anxiety, the feeling of hopelessness was overwhelming:

'I just felt like a piece of shit. I just felt like I was achieving nothing. I couldn't do anything; I was completely stuck and no jobs were coming up, and I just felt so depressed. Every day, I was crying; I was, like, "I hate it". Hated it. Absolutely hated it. I thought I am just the most unemployable person ever, and I was, like, "I can't, I can't do anything." I was at rock bottom actually; it was horrible.' (Interview 10)

Jasmine did manage to find employment, though not at graduate level. She once again took a job in the care sector, utilizing her NVQ Level 3 qualification, rather than her degree. When interviewed, she had a job as a support worker in a day-care centre, paying £16,500 a year. She said she quite enjoyed the work, but the centre was struggling with funding cuts:

'Transport budget has been slashed and we've now got a quarter of what we had last year, and they've already spent it, and this is April-to-April financial year and they've already spent it, and it's July. So, yeah, so we're fucked really; we're borrowing money out of, like, the cleaning budget … just so they can go out, you know, but we can't go any further than the local town, basically, and surrounding areas. Yeah, I don't know how it's going to stay open.' (Interview 10)

While Jasmine felt confident that she could find another job as a low-paid care worker, in her final interview, she also described graphically the tough nature of this type of work, for which nothing at university had prepared her:

'So, care has a smell, and I'm absolutely going to stand by that. And I had this woman, the second call, it was like 7.30 in the morning, and she has, like, fully fledged dementia, completely gone bless her. … She was now back to being, like, completely childlike. And I was helping her have some yogurt, and she was sat up, she'd been bed bound for, like, ten years. … University can't teach you the vulnerability of people. And I was so shocked by that situation. And she was, like, lying there in her bed, and I was feeding her yogurt, and she was just going, "Yah …", like, screaming in my face, "I want my mum; I want my mum". She was like 90-odd, so, obviously, her mum hadn't been around for years, but she was a child again. I put yogurt in her mouth, "Oh, that's nice", and she's screaming in your face, "You fucking bitch; you fucking piece of shit − ooh, that's nice." And she was, like, smearing her shit all over the walls, and I was, like, "What the fuck? I hate care work." And I was, like, "I'm not going back; I can't go back, cannot go back." But I carried on. … I've now seen it all.' (Interview 10)

Despite these experiences, Jasmine clung to some aspirations: to find a place of her own to live; to find work helping deprived children; perhaps to marry her latest boyfriend; and to have fun with friends. She also clung on to her craving to travel: "I do really want to go to America. I do also really want to go to, like, Thailand, Bali, those sorts of places. I would like to go to Asia; just so many places" (Interview 10). However, she was not sure that she would ever have a graduate job. Her narrative highlights strongly the 'emotional and relational work involved in making university-to-work transitions meaningful' (Finn, 2017: 427). Despite being plagued by anxiety and uncertainty, Jasmine is still following aspects of the graduate dream; however, such optimism as she retains lays her open to more heartbreak, characterized by Berlant (2006, 2011) as 'cruel optimism':

> 'Cruel optimism' names a relation of attachment to compromised conditions of possibility. What is cruel

about these attachments, and not merely inconvenient or tragic, is that the subjects who have *x* in their lives might not well endure the loss of their object or scene of desire, even though its presence threatens their well-being, because whatever the *content* of the attachment, the continuity of the form of it provides something of the continuity of the subject's sense of what it means to keep on living on and to look forward to being in the world. (Berlant, 2006: 21, emphasis in original)

Jasmine's narrative epitomizes 'cruel optimism'. She arrives at university with hopes and dreams, and believes in the promise of social mobility through higher education. She dreams of a secure, stable middle-class life, with a steady career doing something of value to society, a dream she optimistically clings to even when the reality of the labour market delivers multiple blows and she finds herself working incredibly hard for very little reward. Her first job as a care worker in Manchester, looking after elderly people, was not a graduate job, but at least fulfilled her criteria of doing work that is of social value. The care-work industry in the UK is a privatized industry that mostly employs working-class women on low pay and is widely regarded as a low-skilled occupation, despite calls from the caring profession to recognize the actual skills of the work that they do. Jasmine found the work hard and moved to a job as a mental health support worker with convicted women, again a low-paid and not a graduate job, where she engages in NVQ-level training, which is important for progression within the job. An NVQ Level 3 is equivalent to A-level qualifications, and Jasmine's degree carries no currency in the area of work she pursues. She is initially enthusiastic about this job and talks about how much she "love[s] making a difference to people's lives". We see snippets of hope and fulfilment, which feed her 'magnetic attraction to cruel optimism, with its suppression of the risks of attachment' (Berlant, 2006: 35). Over time, however, this hope fades to disillusionment as the stress of the job and the reality of expensive city living on low wages impact on her mental health, leading her to "jack her life in" and return home.

On her return home, we see a shift in Jasmine's optimistic outlook as she starts to reckon with the idea that she wants more. Her feelings of hopelessness are palpable in her description of that period – "I just felt like a piece of shit" – and it seems that, for a while, she is jolted into a reality that almost recognizes the fallacy of cruel optimism and a detachment from the dream. We see feelings of despondency, as she believes herself "unemployable", which eventually becomes resignation to what she sees as the reality of her labour market future. In her final interview where she graphically describes the reality of care work, she finishes with the following reflection: "I've now seen it all. Like, from that day onwards, I have seen it all, I have been called everything, I've had people, like, slashing their wrists in front of me. So, there's nothing that life can't throw at me now" (Interview 10).

Jasmine's story was painful to hear, especially as over a period of seven years, we saw the decline of her initial hope. As an undergraduate, Jasmine presented as an enthusiastic, socially aware, smart and energetic working-class young woman, but the labour market did not support her career ambitions or value her potential. Instead, she was metaphorically crushed as she attempted to find work that she valued. In doing so, we see how she comes to accept her life not as the one she planned or hoped for, but as one she can handle. Her narrative resonates with those of working-class young women in research elsewhere, as the outcome 'is neither the end of the world, nor what she had envisaged for herself' (Finn, 2017: 427). While gaining a degree is seen as providing the best chance of success, in reality, she has been unable to mobilize the cultural capital of her degree qualification. In her case, a university education has been unable to deliver on the promise of social mobility, and cases like hers call into question the social mobility agenda, which largely focuses on raising aspirations. Jasmine did not lack aspirations; rather, she lacked labour market opportunity, and her experiences powerfully illustrate the argument that 'social mobility is not, and cannot be, the solution to class inequality' (Ingram and Gamsu, 2022). The difference between Jasmine's early labour market experiences and Martin's (outlined next) throws class and gender inequalities into sharp relief.

Martin's story: escape routes and meaningful futures

'My dad's a clinical consultant psychologist, so he's on a decent wage, quite middle class. He came from quite

a middle-class background in Haringey, my mum,
though, from quite a poor background in Hungary,
living in quite low levels of poverty before coming to the
UK. I'd describe myself as a middle-class background.
Schooling probably would replicate that. I went to quite
a nice Church of England school and then, like, an old
grammar school in Camden.' (Interview 1)

Martin (white, middle class) studied sociology at the UoB. His
introductory description of himself as an undergraduate is indicative
of a certain degree of self-confidence and ease about the future,
which is further exemplified in comments like the following:

'I think I'll probably come out of uni and just find any
job and then just probably work up, not necessarily pick
a career, but let the career pick me. And I think that's
something that I feel quite strongly: that there is more
to life than just following the path and making money
and settling down with a family.' (Interview 3)

The idea of letting a career pick him is quite a striking one that
highlights both Martin's lack of concern for his future and lack of the
need for a plan. Like Jasmine, Martin had progressed to university
unsure of what career he wished to pursue. As with Jasmine, the
desire to travel featured strongly in his narrative, and he had taken
a gap year, typical of many middle-class school leavers, travelling
to America, Thailand, Singapore and Malaysia, while in his second
year, he went with a group of volunteers on an aid-work project
in Uganda. He was one of the few participants in the Paired Peers
project who was strongly political, and he attended left-wing
meetings and was a member of Amnesty International. During his
studies, he also worked in the Big Issue office and was a volunteer at
a shelter for homeless people. These activities and interests informed
his thinking about his career as he ended his second year:

'I'm, kind of, thinking either maybe social research
… or, like, international development or third sector,
so, like, working with charities or something. I never
really was that interested in making like loads of money.

Obviously, I want enough to be comfortable in life, but I'd rather do something that I feel is, like, fulfilling and that I can see my work being used in a good way and trying to improve society. Social research, I think, is a really good way of understanding what are the problems in societies and where the inequalities are, so that's why I'm thinking social research because that's quite a good mechanism for emancipation. But I'm also quite interested in, like, human rights and international development because a lot of, like, these problems are unequal to the Western world's advantage. And I really like travelling and seeing, learning more about other cultures, so that, kind of, ties in, like, international development.' (Interview 4)

Martin's "obvious" desire to be comfortably off was supported by the knowledge that his family could provide a buffer zone to cushion him from the need to pursue a graduate career immediately:

'My vague plan is to, like, move back home and get any job and just save up and then move away, go travelling, see the rest of the world, which will kind of defer my career progression, so I won't need to worry about it. I didn't mind moving back home because, you know, that's the reality, and I know very few people that haven't had to move home after graduating; that's just kind of what everyone has to do now, unfortunately, because jobs are so tough and it takes a while to get one, and rent is ridiculous, especially in London.' (Interview 6)

Whereas Jasmine's path post-graduation was filled with struggle and hardship, Martin was in a position to make the most of a range of different opportunities that came his way. He first had an unpaid internship for three months with the Red Cross, where community experience is required. To earn money, he worked in a bar in the evening.

He then gained a job as an office manager for a small charity. While the job was good CV material and offered him opportunities for travel to Africa on field visits, he became bored with what he described as "basically office work" (Interview 7). After a year, he quit and set out to travel, confident to face the risks he had identified prior to taking his job with the charity:

'I was, kind of, thinking maybe I should just go travelling cos that's, kind of, what, like, my passion is, but I guess again that fear of, like, running away and not having anything to come back to, and then needing a job and an income, meant that I, kind of, started looking. And what I'm interested in, like, international development and charity work, is really, really competitive. So, I just, I erm, like, applied to a load of jobs and, erm, after a few months, I got lucky.' (Interview 8)

There followed two years packed with incident: he flew to Russia; travelled on the Trans-Siberian Express; bought a motorbike; and travelled around China and Vietnam. Settling in Saigon, he met people who advised him that he could get a job as an English teacher, so he applied: "There's a very high demand for 'native' English teachers, as they call it, hence why I got a job so easily even though I didn't have any qualifications or any visas or anything" (Interview 9). After teaching for a while, he felt restless again and set off to Australia and other countries for a year of what he described as "travelling/work, travelling/work, travelling/work", before returning to Vietnam for another spell of teaching:

'I was enjoying it, but I, kind of, felt like it was getting a bit, like, unfulfilling, like, discovering that, like, money isn't going to run out because I can just stop and work; it's not as difficult as it seems in the UK. So, I decided to move back to Vietnam. As well, like, my girlfriend was also, like, unsure what to do, and she wanted to work, and so we both decided to go to Hanoi. We thought, "OK, let's just go to this place and stop and, like, make a life there, and then work out what we want to do long term" because at least there, we know that we can get work to, like, support ourselves while we plan the rest – and as well, there's a lot of NGOs [non-governmental organizations] based in Hanoi.' (Interview 9)

Once again, Martin became bored with teaching, and the opportunities with NGOs did not materialize; what did come up was a one-year contract for work in Malta with a European Union (EU)-funded organization rescuing migrant refugees from the Mediterranean. The work was temporary and paid only at the level of living expenses but fitted with Martin's political ideals and, importantly, allowed him to realize his ambitions and to live the graduate life that he valued. Martin described his role:

> 'I work in logistics and planning. ... Making sure that we have, like, the food and the kind of clothes and the space blankets and the medicine and the medical team to run the operation, trying to, like, procure them and trying to plan what we need and where it needs to go, and then how it can get on to the boats.' (Interview 10)

Martin's life post-graduation, as shown here, is characterized by a churn and precarity that might appear to be similar to Jasmine's. In order to make real progress in his chosen field of international development, he would need further qualifications, and he currently lacked the resources to fund a master's degree. His observation was that most people who have progressed in the field come from wealthy families, enabling them to gain a couple of years' experience as unpaid volunteers or interns out in the field, in Africa or South America, and then complete a master's, all at the family's expense. In his final interview, Martin reflected on the instability of his working life and suggested an unknown future, albeit one that could be cushioned by family capital and accommodation in London, which can itself facilitate opportunity and success, as discussed in Chapter 3:

> 'My economic situation is very precarious; like, I don't have any stability, and in a year's time, I have no idea where I'll be. ... Even though I have now quite a bit of experience and quite a bit of an idea for what I'm interested in, there's not much work. So, yeah, I could

be back in London … trying to get any job while I live in my mum's house.' (Interview 10)

Precarity or privilege?

Despite not fitting narrow definitions of success as measured by income, Martin's story shows how he is in a position to take advantage of a range of opportunities that are not part of a clear graduate career path, but that he can construct as steps towards a future because he has sufficient family back-up and security, and enough middle-class confidence, to do so. It is interesting to consider how the work that he engaged in within international development and the charitable sector is valued within a middle-class milieu. Many would recognize this as worthy graduate work, and indeed many people employed in international development are graduates. Yet, his work is poorly remunerated, which has consequences when thinking about the conversion of capital. At this point in his career, Martin is not converting his symbolic capital into economic capital, and it is not clear if he will succeed in this. However, his familial economic capital allows him to make decisions outside of homogeneous representations of 'successful' adulthood (Jeffrey, 2010), converting economic to cultural capital in the form of skills and knowledge for operating in a globalizing world (Frandberg, 2014; Cairns, 2015). Here, we see an inversion of the expected graduate capital conversion of cultural to economic. While not currently lucrative, Martin's international development work carries significant symbolic capital, which may later be traded for more remunerative employment within the field. Martin was aware of the links between the experiences he had been accruing with a well-trodden alternative career pathway that is often dominated by those from privileged backgrounds. Securing a career in this field requires a navigation of precarity, sporadic low-paid and unpaid employment/internships, and the cost of international travel, all of which require a significant investment of economic capital.

In many ways, then, what might be characterized as precarity turns out to be the flexibility available through the workings of privilege. Martin has been able to launch himself into an insecure world of global geographical mobility without acknowledging concern for things not working out. His narrative shows that what can be characterized as 'precarity' holds different meanings for people from different social class backgrounds. Precarity can be risk-free for people like Martin, who have family capital to fall back on. Indeed, his decision to travel, explore and try out different forms of employment is relatively risk-free, as his fallback position would be to return to London to find work. If he fails in some endeavour, there is always the 'escape route' of return to the family home open to him, plus his experience of teaching offers another possible line of escape. In the meantime, the work that Martin has accessed across different nation states allows him to develop forms of 'global cultural capital' (Kim, 2011), characterized by geopolitical knowledge of different contexts and flexible geographic mobility.

In terms of future employability, these capitals are highly valued in the context of global cosmopolitan futures (Skrbis et al, 2014), and Martin's flexibility, mobility and propensity to navigate precarity position him as a model global graduate, even though he has not yet secured a recognized graduate job. Courtois (2020: 240) argues that the discourse of mobility 'converges with that of flexibility and entrepreneurialism, by treating as obsolete expectations of stability and security and by framing individuals as self-reliant, dis-embedded and "free" (in fact, expected) to relocate as required or desired in the global labour market'. Martin's precarity or instability may, then, be convertible to global cultural capital, which has currency in elite graduate labour markets.

Transnational mobility also affords Martin the opportunity to live a life that has meaning to him and to construct a non-linear pathway that is free from the necessity of securing highly paid graduate work and a known and predictable future. In relation to the generational increase of young people 'on the move', Robertson et al (2018: 207) argue that:

> Its effects and meanings beyond ... [an] instrumental function tend to be overlooked, especially the broader implications for youth who are not simply pursuing better job prospects, but are effectively making a social and civic life on the move and negotiating belonging, place attachment and new imaginings of adulthood, settledness and futurity in the process.

Martin has the right volume and composition of capitals to orientate him towards the choice of travel, and he is able to convert both his economic capital (which may be latent and manifest in security) and cultural capital into a post-university journey that positively shapes his sense of his graduate self, and to negotiate his own meanings of a graduate life, which are not dependent on securing a graduate career. His embodied cultural capital and middle-class confidence allow him to make risky choices that it is very unlikely would be readily taken up by working-class graduates, such as Ruby and Leo, whose stories are told elsewhere in this book, and for whom security was a crucial goal.

Conclusion

While the stories of Jasmine and Martin share similarities in terms of aspirations for work that makes a difference and their experience of low-paid labour, their narratives stand in stark contrast to one another and allow us to explore intersectional classed and gendered graduate labour market transitions. We have chosen them both as examples of contrasting classed processes of struggle and ease in labour market transitions, and as a means of demonstrating the important role of capital conversion in securing a graduate life. They both left university with good degree outcomes in the discipline of sociology, with dreams of a bright future. The four years post-graduation allowed Martin to explore work options in the international development sector and to travel, accruing global cultural capital, while carving a symbolically recognized graduate pathway that aligned with his personal ambitions and social values. In parallel, Jasmine accrued a range of experiences within the care industry, a feminized and classed section of the labour market. While this initially satisfied her personal goals of doing socially useful work, she ended up on a pathway of non-graduate employment. She had to retrain and acquire a Level 3 NVQ qualification (equivalent to a university entrance-level qualification), and suffered from living a tough existence associated both with the conditions of her labour (zero-hours contracts and exploitative work) and with poor financial reward. Jasmine's descriptions of her day-to-day experiences of work are harrowing, and the trauma of the work impacts on her mental health. This contrasts with Martin's experience, which involves work at the logistical level, rather than on the front line. In their narratives, we can see differences in the way in which they are able to convert capitals. Martin is able to utilize his family economic capital to generate the conditions in which travel is possible and to minimize the risk to his sense of graduate self or graduate future by engaging in activity that is both meaningful to him and recognized as something that graduates do. In this way, he is able to convert both his economic capital and his cultural capital into symbolic capital in the form of global cultural capital. Jasmine, by contrast, is unable to convert the capital she has acquired. Her institutionalized cultural capital in the form of a degree qualification proves difficult to mobilize in a hostile graduate labour market, and she cannot take the same decisions to gain meaningful experiences through transnational mobility that Martin can. Instead, she is constrained to make choices within the limitations of local labour markets, which, in the end, fail to deliver opportunities and offer considerable suffering and precarity.

Peter Kelly (2017: 68) argues that 'we may be condemning generations of young people to a life-long experience of precariousness and debt'. This chapter highlights how precarity is experienced and navigated differently depending on social class and, in particular, the availability of economic capital, whether that is financial assistance or the buffer provided by the security of the option of returning home for a period of time. The difference between Jasmine's and Martin's prospects of returning home are that one is a defeat, for an indefinite period, and not perceived as a basis for moving forward, while the other is an opportunity to pause and redirect energies.

The challenge that their very different experiences present is that taking a degree no longer leads easily into economic security and success. Many graduates will fail to realize their dreams in unfavourable graduate labour market conditions. Nonetheless, when we questioned the graduates in the Paired Peers study, very few regretted having taken a degree. Instead, many of them talked of how it helped them to mature and become more self-reliant, and they appreciated the friendships they had made and the fun of their social lives. Moreover, many felt that their appreciation of their discipline had deepened, and quite a few wanted to continue to gain further academic qualifications. Others spoke of how being at university had broadened their horizons and taught them about the lives of people from different backgrounds. Loveday (2014: 581) movingly quotes a working-class mature student she interviewed as saying that his higher education experience allowed him 'to become the person I was always meant to be'. Being a graduate, therefore, goes beyond a simple narrow economistic conception of work and encompasses a humanistic value: the opportunities to develop knowledge and capacity for critique, expand minds, and promote civilization. A degree can be seen as a means to support people to live a life that they value and has meaning to them, which is an expectation and aspiration that unifies many graduates, and is something that our study supports – many young people felt optimism for their futures at the point of graduation.

However, the labour market is not structured to reward those who wish to choose otherwise in their search for meaningful work, so that for those without the cushion of family financial support, cruel optimism prevails in the 'compromised conditions of possibility' (Berlant, 2006: 21). This chapter has shown how aspiration and capital accumulation are not enough to ensure successful labour market transitions. In Jasmine's case, symbolic closure has been generated through 'cruel optimism', as her aspirations for meaningful work are delegitimated by society's shared ideas of what constitutes valued graduate activity.

Jasmine's narrative is a classic case of cruel optimism, heartbreak and broken dreams, despite the resilience she shows in chasing opportunities. However, Martin's narrative may also show aspects of cruel optimism. In the post-COVID-19 world of increasing precarity, diminishing stable occupations and increasing global tensions, he may never be able to convert his global cultural capital into the kind of development work he hopes to secure. Those from the middle class of the degree generation are not immune from the breaking of dreams.

References

Atkinson, W. and Bradley, H. (2013) Ordinary lives: class reproduction and everyday practice in contemporary Britain, ESRC, https://data.bris.ac.uk/data/dataset/9830c9701956b0c73412134f6aa318d1

Bathmaker, A.M., Ingram, N., Abrahams, J., Hoare, A., Waller, R. and Bradley, H. (2016) *Higher Education, Social Class and Social Mobility: The Degree Generation*, London: Palgrave Macmillan.

Berlant, L. (2006) Cruel optimism, *Differences: A Journal of Feminist Cultural Studies*, 17(5): 21.

Berlant, L. (2011) *Cruel Optimism*, Durham, NC: Duke University Press.

Berlant, L. (2019) Why chasing the good life is holding us back, with Lauren Berlant, https://humanities.uchicago.edu/articles/2019/11/why-chasing-good-life-holding-us-back-lauren-berlant

Boliver, V. (2011) Expansion, differentiation, and the persistence of social class inequalities in British higher education, *Higher Education*, 61: 229–42.

Bourdieu, P. (1986) The forms of capital, in J. Richardson (ed) *Handbook of Theory and Research for the Sociology of Education*, Westport, CT: Greenwood, pp 241–58.

Brooks, R. and Everett, G. (2008) 'The prevalence of life planning': evidence from UK graduates, *British Journal of Sociology of Education*, 29(3): 325–37.

Brown, P. (1999) Globalization and the political economy of high skills, *Journal of Education and Work*, 12(3): 233–51.

Brown, P. (2003) The opportunity trap: education and employment in a global economy, *European Educational Research Journal*, 2(1): 141–79.

Brown, P., Lauder, H. and Ashton, D. (2011) *The Global Auction: The Broken Promises of Education, Jobs and Income*, Oxford: Oxford University Press.

Brown, P., Lauder, H. and Cheung, S.Y. (2020) *The Death of Human Capital? Its Failed Promise and How to Renew It in an Age of Disruption*, Oxford: Oxford University Press.

Cairns, D.C. (2015) Mapping the youth mobility field, in A. Lange, C. Steiner, S. Schutter and H. Reiter (eds) *Handbook of Child and Youth Sociology*, Wiesbaden: Springer, pp 1–16.

Courtois, A. (2020) Study abroad as governmentality: the construction of hypermobile subjectivities in higher education, *Journal of Education Policy*, 35(2): 237–57.

DfES (Department for Education and Skills) (1991) *Higher Education: A New Framework*, London: HMSO.

Finn, K. (2017) Relational transitions, emotional decisions: new directions for theorising graduate employment, *Journal of Education and Work*, 30(4): 419–31.

Frandberg, L. (2014) Temporary transnational youth migration and its mobility links, *Mobilities*, 9(1): 146–64.

Friedman, S. and Laurison, D. (2020) *The Class Ceiling*, Bristol: Policy Press.

Goldthorpe, J.H. (2016) Social class mobility in modern Britain: changing structure, constant process, *Journal of the British Academy*, 4: 89–111.

Harrison, N. and Waller, R. (2018) Challenging discourses of aspiration: the role of expectations and attainment in access to higher education, *British Education Research Journal*, 44(5): 914–38.

Ingram, N. and Allen, K. (2019) 'Talent-spotting' or 'social magic'? Inequality, cultural sorting and constructions of the ideal graduate in elite professions, *The Sociological Review*, 67(3): 723–40.

Ingram, N. and Gamsu, S. (2022) Talking the talk of social mobility: the political performance of a misguided agenda, *Sociological Research Online*, https://doi.org/10.1177/13607804211055493

Jeffrey, C. (2010) Geographies of children and youth I: eroding maps of life, *Progress in Human Geography*, 34(4): 496–505.

Kelly, P. (2017) Growing up after the GFC: responsibilization and mortgaged futures, *Discourse*, 38(1): 57–69.

Kim, J. (2011) Global cultural capital and global positional competition: international graduate students' transnational occupational trajectories, *British Journal of Sociology of Education*, 37(1): 30–50.

Loveday, V. (2014) Working-class participation, middle-class aspiration? Value, upward mobility and symbolic indebtedness in higher education, *The Sociological Review*, 63(3): 570–88.

Milburn, A. (2009) *Unleashing Aspirations: Final Report of the Panel on Fair Access to the Professions*, London: Cabinet Office.

Milburn, A. (2012a) *Fair Access to Professional Careers: Report by Independent Reviewer on Social Mobility and Child Poverty*, London: Cabinet Office.

Milburn, A. (2012b) *University Challenge: How Higher Education Can Advance Social Mobility*, London: Assets Publishing Service, https://assets.publishing.service.gov.uk/government/uploads/system/uploads/attachment_data/file/80188/Higher-Education.pdf

Public Accounts Committee (2009) *Widening Participation in Higher Education: Fourth Report of Session 2008–2009*, London: House of Commons Stationery Office Limited, https://publications.parliament.uk/pa/cm200809/cmselect/cmpubacc/226/9780215526557.pdf

Purcell, K., Elias, P., Atfield, G., Behle, H., Ellison, R. and Luchinskaya, D. (2013) *Transitions into Employment, Further Study and Other Outcomes: The Futuretrack Stage 4 Report*, Manchester and Coventry: HECSU and Warwick Institute for Employment Research.

Reay, D. (2017) *Miseducation*, Bristol: Policy Press.

Robertson, S., Harris, A. and Baldassar, L. (2018) Mobile transitions: a conceptual framework for researching a generation on the move, *Journal of Youth Studies*, 21(2): 203–17.

Skrbis, Z., Woodward, I. and Bean, C. (2014) Seeds of cosmopolitan future?, *Journal of Youth Studies*, 17(5): 614–25.

Social Mobility Commission (2019) *State of the Nation 2018–19: Social Mobility in Great Britain*, London: Social Mobility Commission, www.gov.uk/government/publications/social-mobility-in-great-britain-state-of-the-nation-2018-to-2019

Walkerdine, V., Lucey, H. and Melody, J. (2001) *Growing Up Girl: Psychosocial Explorations of Gender and Class*, Basingstoke: Palgrave.

Waller, R., Holford, J., Jarvis, P., Milana, M. and Webb, S. (2014) Widening participation, social mobility and the role of universities in a globalized world, *International Journal of Lifelong Education*, 33(6): 701–4.

8

Lucky Breaks? Unplanned Graduate Pathways and Fateful Outcomes

Introduction

In this chapter, we turn to a consideration of graduate pathways for those who had no clear and definite employment plan during their time at university and at the point of exit. In doing so, we consider the ways in which early experiences of transition from university are inflected by social class, race and gender. The chapter presents the narratives of two middle-class, white, male politics graduates – Oscar and Liam – and two working-class history graduates – one white male (Garry) and one 'mixed-race' (white Welsh and African-Caribbean heritage) female (Adele). We consider the development of their career pathways on leaving university and highlight the significance of the role of time in facilitating/shutting down opportunity. We compare the unplanned 'serendipity' of the middle-class graduates with the unplanned 'fateful outcomes' of their working-class counterparts. The chapter highlights that what can superficially appear to be luck or serendipity is, in fact, a manifestation of privilege and relies on the availability of stocks of capital. Moreover, outcomes that appear to be 'fateful' are actually mediated by classed, racialized and gendered forms of capital. The chapter concludes with consideration of graduate spaces as important components in the navigation of unplanned pathways in the ways in which they invite privileged bodies, while rendering 'other' bodies as trespassers (Puwar, 2004).

Like many UK graduates across higher education, there were a number of young people in our study who graduated with minimal plans for the immediate future and no clear employment pathway. We found no pattern in terms of strategic planning and institution attended, gender, or class or ethnic background. We did, however, discern that certain subjects, such as law, economics, engineering, accounting and finance, were more likely to produce graduates with direct career goals. It is obvious that these subjects are taken with particular careers in mind, and this observation is not surprising. However, in the current context where some university subjects are under fire for their apparent lack of employment opportunities, it is important for us to highlight that a significant number of graduates taking subjects that do not have an obvious employment outcome go on to develop successful graduate careers. It is also important to note that many of these successes happen without the intervention of institutions' careers services and employability initiatives. In this chapter, we consider four such graduates and their smooth and fractious transitions from university to employment, shedding light on the process of following a minimally planned pathway and the ways in which class, ethnicity and gender intersect to generate conditions for luck, fortune and serendipity.

Unplanned fateful outcomes

In considering how their lives unfold, we are interested in how the young adults' opportunities, obstacles, successes and failures come to be understood within a framework of fate or 'luck'. Loveday (2017: 762) argues that people resort to explanations of luck when they feel they have no control over their situations and that a 'frequent recourse to notions of luck, chance and happenstance … is indicative of … [their] diminished agency'. In this chapter, we likewise show that notions of luck and bad luck are turned to when, in the absence of strategic planning, young people look for explanations for the things that happen to them as their careers unfold. However, while Loveday (2017: 763) maintains that notions of luck 'were not consciously invoked as a way of denying advantage', we argue that luck operates unconsciously as a trope for the misrecognition of privilege or disadvantage. While it is not used deliberately to deny privilege, the wielding of luck obscures structures of advantage. Connected to notions of luck are notions of fate, and in this chapter, we develop the concept of 'unplanned fateful outcomes' in order to consider the unfolding (rather than planning) of lives as a process, or as a series of happenings that are mediated through the habitus in a way that orientates people towards particular pathways and outcomes. We build upon but move beyond Giddens' notion of 'fateful moments': 'Fateful moments are times when events come together in such a way that an individual stands, as it were, at a crossroads in his existence; or where a person learns of information with fateful consequences' (Giddens, 1991: 113).

Our concept of 'unplanned fateful outcomes' does not involve decision making at a crossroads of existence, but rather considers how unplanned pathways are shaped by orientation, rather than choice. In another departure from Giddens, Holland and Thomson (2009) conceive of 'critical moments' as a way of thinking about key junctures and events that steer the direction of the life course. While the idea of a critical moment or event that leads to a juncture where key decisions need to be made is compelling, we are curious to explore what happens when there is no significant critical moment, yet the material circumstances, history of experiences and dispositions elide to orientate a person in a direction that then has a fateful outcome.

The following two sections interrogate ideas about unplanned serendipity and fateful outcomes. We start with a discussion of two middle-class graduates who were 'fortunate' enough to be able to pause and consider their future options before making a graduate career move. We then turn to discuss the transition experiences of two working-class graduates who 'fall into' immediate employment.

Time to get a job? Minimally planned serendipity

Upon leaving university, both Oscar (middle-class, UWE) and Liam (middle-class, UoB) had no immediate plans for starting to work. During their three years of study, they had both toyed with a range of ideas for the direction they might take, but these did not go further than the thinking phase and were not put into any form of strategic action. They both returned home and 'pressed pause'.

In what follows, we expose the ways in which this simple act of pausing operates as a form of 'time capital' (a form of cultural and social capital afforded, ultimately, by economic capital). In both their cases, this 'time capital' interacts with their ability to mobilize familial resources to allow them to 'do the London thing', itself a key catalyst for graduate career success, as shown in Chapter 3. We focus mainly on an exploration of Oscar's experiences of the first four years after graduation, drawing out the complexity of his transition and considering stability and instability, decision making, and chance happenings, as well as turning points and fateful outcomes. Within this analysis, we apply a Bourdieusian class lens to consider the role of habitus and forms of capital in lived processes of transition as a graduate. We then turn to consider Liam and highlight some of the similarities in terms of being able to mobilize capitals to create the favourable conditions for opportunity and luck.

Oscar had minimal plans upon graduation and no clear direction of travel. When we caught up with him at Interview 7, a year after graduation, he explained how he had spent the year working on his drumming (including attending a world conference for the style of music he was immersed in through his father's music teaching and performance business) before deciding that this was not the career path he wished to follow. In returning home, he was not simply hanging around with nothing to do; rather, he saw the period after university as a time for exploration. He was able to invest in something he enjoyed, and this crucially afforded time to think if this could be his way of making a 'career'. He decided it was not, but knowing what he did not want to do did not translate into knowing what he did want to do, and in the absence of direction, he opted to take the path to London – to 'do the London thing'. This is a recognized 'legitimate' graduate pathway, and London is seen as a place of opportunity to develop early graduate careers (see Chapter 3). What is notable about Oscar's move to London is that it was disassociated from securing work. As he explains: "So, by 'the London thing', I just mean be up here really and, kind of, see how it goes. So, I did that but without much of a plan employment-wise" (Interview 7). While he describes this plan to simply uproot and go to London as "wonderfully naive" (Interview 7), it is a plan that he could execute because he was able to draw upon the 'London capital' of his older sister, who had been living and working there after her own graduation. He moved into his sister's house and started to look for graduate jobs. In a sense, his wonderful naivety was, in fact, an expression of his specific volumes and composition of social, cultural and economic capital, linked to his privileged class position. Oscar had some savings, which he had accrued through working for his father and living at home, and could take the 'risk' of moving to London without a job because his sister provided support through accommodation. Despite having the enabling capitals that operated as a buffer to risk, Oscar initially struggled to gain a foothold in the graduate labour market. His initial hopes and optimism soon turned to despair. He described his expectations in the following way: "I thought I'd just, kind of, come up … with a personal interest in politics and a degree to boot, you know; really, it would just be a case of picking from the job offers which would obviously come my way!" (Interview 7). He then went on to articulate the pains of navigating the graduate labour market and applying for graduate schemes:

> 'And like, God, it was pretty bleak at first; I mean, it very quickly becomes apparent that it's just, like, a very horrible environment. I saw some adverts saying, you know, "graduate job opportunities", you know, just, like, a fake kind of advert which said "graduate job opportunity", you know, and the requirements were like three Olympic gold medals or world records.' (Interview 7)

The graduate labour market is an increasingly hostile and unstable space even for middle-class graduates who possess significant social, cultural and economic capital, and Oscar's pathway is a testament to this. However, his narrative also highlights the resilience of class privilege when it encounters hostilities that threaten to destabilize its position in the social field. Oscar's capitals enabled a sojourn of unemployment in London while he navigated the challenging labour market. This allowed him to submit 23 job applications, which resulted in just one interview for a three-month fixed-term contract. The difficulties in securing work were quite confronting for Oscar, who, like many others, left university full of expectation and hope for the future. In the end, through a simple twist of fate (or chance happening), rather than through strategic planning, he secured a position with the London Ambulance Service. The randomness of this accidental good fortune is highlighted in Oscar's explanation of the circumstances of his success:

'My sister, who works as a speech and language therapist, said there was a position for emergency ambulance crew with the London Ambulance Service and was, like, "What about that?" And I read it, and it basically was, like, a basic ambulance driver. And I was like, "Yeah, that would be good, pretty fun", like, jokingly whatever. Put the application together … sent it off, and yeah, I kind of ended up being successful.' (Interview 7)

Despite the appearance of serendipity, chance or good luck in landing on an opportunity that might lead somewhere and is at least regarded as interesting or worthy for the time being, Oscar's success can be read as a manifestation of privilege. He presents his success as a hard-won battle through the "bleak" reality of the labour market and a serendipitous moment of good fortune; yet, when we consider the enabling capitals that afforded the time and space to keep opportunities open to him, it becomes clear that luck, the freedom to wait and the capacity to indulge in being "wonderfully naive" are all a smokescreen for white, male, middle-class privilege. This can be framed as a form of social magic (Ingram and Allen, 2019), where embodied privilege is misrecognized as something outside of the individual. In this case, the exploitation of middle-class capital is magically transformed into luck. Oscar's pathway does not run smoothly, and he faces further setbacks as his life unfolds. He applies to become a paramedic, which would be a step up from ambulance crew, but is unsuccessful in this. However, after working for several years for the London Ambulance Service, he decides that he would like to pursue a medical career, and in the final project interview with Oscar, he was looking into postgraduate medicine degree courses.

We now turn to consider Liam's pathway in order to further exemplify issues of class in the process of transition from higher education. Like Oscar, Liam was also in the position to 'take time out' and use it as a form of capital, but he used time capital in a much more strategic way. As he explains:

> 'I just, sort of, took a bit of time out just at home to decide what I wanted to do. Decided I want to be a lawyer, so just spent time, like, researching that, applying, got a vacation scheme with a firm in April, by end of March, beginning of April, and had, like, an interview at the end of that, and they offered me a job, which consists of two years at law school starting at September 2014, which they sort of pay your fees and they pay you, like, a living grant, tax-free grant, and then a two-year training contract, which will run from September 2016 to September 2018.' (Interview 7)

In Liam's case, he is able to use the time capital in order to make the shift from having no direction to developing a clear strategic plan. He is able to spend the first ten months following graduation to carefully consider and research his options, rather than having to respond to whatever opportunity comes along (in contrast to Oscar earlier). He tells us that the research he did was positive and led him to explore his options further by embarking on additional fact-finding about the job through a "vacation scheme". This led him to an important turning point, where he made the decision about the road he wanted to travel: "A couple of days into the vacation scheme, only one as it turned out, I decided, 'Yeah, this is for me; everything feels right', and also the firm, in particular, felt right. So, when they offered me a job, I just took it – and that was it" (Interview 7).

Liam's transition is similar to Oscar's in terms of the important role of time in affording the opportunity to explore options. While Liam's transition is somewhat smoother, stable and more considered than Oscar's, they both made decisions 'within their culturally derived horizons for action' (Hodkinson and Sparkes, 1997: 41), which engendered the privilege of an open outlook and an expansive opportunity-scape. Through waiting, thinking, exploring, researching and trying, they each, in their own way, found a path they wanted to pursue. In these cases, we see how fortune and opportunity are therefore made possible through middle-class privilege, where time becomes a catalyst for capital.

Unplanned fateful outcomes: falling into work

The graduate pathways followed by Oscar and Liam stand in strong contrast to the experiences of Adele and Garry, working-class students who had to navigate their career futures without the time to pause. Upon leaving university, Adele continued with a job she had secured during the course of her degree after completing a paid internship. She was working as a fund-raising officer for a small charity in Bristol, and upon graduation, they offered her a full-time position. It was not necessarily the job she aspired to do, but earning money was important to her, as her family did not have the economic capital to support her while she waited for the right opportunity to present itself, or for her to explore and consider her options. It was taken for granted that she would support herself, and she did not entertain the possibility of not working. This was a common position among the working-class young people in our study. While she felt "lucky" that she had a job that she liked, she also recognized that in not taking time to pause, she was closing herself off to other possibilities, such as travel. Her framing of this transition as both good and bad luck is interesting to consider:

> 'I was just here continuing on with my job, which I really enjoyed and I really liked, and I was quite lucky in the fact that I … unlucky and lucky: lucky that I had a job that I could go into which I liked and that paid; unlucky in the fact that maybe I didn't really, kind of, have time to have a break, go travelling, really kind of discover what I wanted to do. … So, it's kind of weird, I don't know how I ended up in the charity sector; I was just, kind of, like. … I don't understand how it happened; I just, kind of, like … I obviously just got lucky. I didn't get lucky, because I did work my arse off in that internship and then they offered me a full-time job.' (Interview 7)

Adele frames her employment success as luck but recognizes the significance of her own hard work in its securement. Her discussion of this luck and opportunity is somewhat ambivalent, tainted by not being able to have a break and, crucially, not having time and space to "discover". Her acceptance of her job is presented as settling for the 'right now', rather than the 'right job', what Bourdieu refers to as 'the choice of the necessary'. Adele presents it as a non-choice, as something that just happened and that she does not fully understand. This carries through into subsequent years, and in an interview three years after graduation, she maintains: "I never, kind of, thought I was going to be a corporate fund-raiser; I feel like that was, kind of, chosen for me and I, kind of, slotted in, and now I can't get out – but I quite like it as well; it's really odd" (Interview 9). Adele's framing of her career path as something that was "chosen for" her, rather than a choice she definitively made, is an interesting example of boundaried decision making (Goldthorpe, 2007; Glaesser and Cooper, 2013). Instead of choosing from a suite of options, Adele's 'choice' of direction is guided by her everyday existence, or her 'periods of routine' (Hodkinson and Sparkes, 1997), which provide a general orientation, rather than a roadmap of pathways to choose from.

Like many of the working-class participants, Adele is not afforded the luxury of time to be strategic about launching her graduate career (for further discussion of time and stopgaps, see Ingram et al, 2018), and she is not presented with a range of pathways and choices. The parameters of her horizons for action (Hodkinson and Sparkes, 1997) are delineated by her class position. She has high ambitions for success in terms of both salary and status (she uses phrases like, "I'm going to go up"), and over the period of the first four years post-graduation in which we followed her, she articulates frustration with what she perceives as the lack of challenge afforded by her position. Despite this, she is always quick to highlight the positive aspects, like the people she works with, and often refers to her 'luck' in having employment at all:

> 'Although it's not challenging me, I am happy. I'm not going to work, like, "Oh, God, I hate it", and I've been lucky enough to not being stuck for work since I left university; I've gone straight into work and haven't left.

I'm just at that stage where I, kind of, want to develop a bit more and possibly go on to do something else in the charitable sector. But I do think I'm on the right track, I just don't know how long that track is and where the end point is, and I, kind of, think, you know, it's not a race and I'm just, kind of, grappling with that and trying to not beat myself up for, you know, perhaps not earning more or not being in a higher position.' (Interview 8)

Adele's luck presents as gratitude, which contrasts with some of the middle-class students' sense of entitlement to graduate employment (Abrahams, 2019). However, her interviews over the four years convey her yearning for something more and her feeling that she is not being stretched. Adele, a working-class, mixed-race woman from a post-92 university, struggles to find her way to the fulfilling job she desires and is qualified for, while many of her white, middle-class male counterparts enjoy success and challenge in jobs that they are not technically qualified for (see, for example, Luke in Chapter 3).

Garry also left university without a plan for his career. From a working-class background, he left the UoB with a 2:1 in history. The following year, when asked the extent to which he considered himself to have planned his career, Garry responded with the following:

'Not at all, not even slightly. Well, certainly not up until two years ago. *I fell into my first job* post-university working as a customer service adviser for Bristol City Council, no … purely pragmatic, not remotely interesting, there was no career plan, no trajectory, and then applying for graduate schemes left, right and centre, there was a real variety of different schemes I was applying for, anything from finance, to teaching, to law, to what I ultimately got. And then I think I went into this role without any real understanding of what project management was as a discipline or what it involved.' (Interview 10)

Garry's lack of planning is striking, as is his pragmatic approach to simply finding a job on a graduate scheme regardless of the scheme's underlying focus. He claims to have fallen into his first appointment, which echoes Adele's sentiments about her career being "chosen for" her. Both of these young people do not feel that they have been active agents in choosing their career paths. Garry's first job is taken through necessity and fear of not finding anything else later. As he explains:

> 'I'd only, sort of, speculatively applied for a few entry-level things whilst exams were going on because I thought I might as well, see what happens. And I was so shocked to actually find something and get something that quickly, I thought, "If I turn that down because I want a bit more of, like, a gap year and then I just don't find anything for ages, I'll kick myself" because that's … you know, it's in Bristol, the money obviously wasn't fantastic, but it was reasonable for what I needed.' (Interview 7)

Like Adele, he took the 'right now' job despite it not inspiring him with joy, and like Adele, he recognized how this shut down possibilities for taking time out, whether to enjoy a 'gap' year or to spend time thinking about what career future he would like to pursue. Garry did not find his job challenging, and in interviews, he spoke of boredom and described the thought of being stuck there as "ridiculous and depressing" (Interview 8). In response to this lack of fulfilment, he became "more determined to really step up the applications for grad schemes" and had a number of knockbacks before getting to the final stages of interview for a job in Edinburgh. At this point, he had decided to cast his net more widely than the surrounding Bristol area. When his interview was unsuccessful, he felt further "disheartened" (Interview 8). Garry's early labour market experiences are fraught with struggles and involve a form of insecurity that comes from feeling unsettled, rather than not having a graduate job. This unsettledness is connected to both a lack of plan/direction and having a job that, on the face of it, looks like secure graduate work but, in reality, leaves him aspiring for an unknown something more. Eventually, Garry is motivated by his own boredom to persuade his manager to let him develop schemes and projects that stimulated him and utilized his skill set:

'So, then a position came up on a gradate scheme at consultancy company, and there were lots of different streams you could apply for, and one was project management. And basically, where I'd pestered my line manager at City Council to be given a bit more … even though there was no capacity for a higher-paid position or anything, I'd become like the technical trainer on the team, and so, basically, I was devising, like, training schemes and projects for new starters on teams that … for no extra money, but I just was just bored, and I wanted time off the phones and facing people, basically.' (Interview 8)

After a year of struggling to get onto another graduate scheme, Garry finally had success and landed a job with a large company working as an IT project manager. While it was not part of any sort of grand scheme for his life, he found the work engaging and challenging. Looking back on his pathway four years after graduation, he reflected:

'Project manager. So, it's one of those wonderful modern meaningless job titles that doesn't really convey a sense of anything that I need to do day to day, but, yeah, I've largely fallen into IT project management, which is, when I look back on where I was three years ago, is a bit ridiculous, history graduate and all.' (Interview 10)

Even with hindsight, Garry is unable to construct his pathway as planned or as something that makes sense. Again, he invokes the idea of falling into it. He has clearly made decisions, but at the same time, his transition can be characterized by a lack of clarity of purpose or overall vision. On the one hand, he is aspirational, but on the other hand, he is unable to articulate the shape of that aspiration. He makes his decisions within his horizons for action, the parameters of which are constrained by the class-related opportunity structures of graduate labour markets, as well as class-related knowledge of labour market opportunities. Garry's trajectory highlights the ways in which 'class-inflected uncertainties, insecurities and fears influenced the unfolding of careers' (Bathmaker, 2021: 86).

Finding the 'right' place

Having a lucky break in navigating a graduate career can also be read as being fortunate enough to find the 'right' place, a place to belong and in which to flourish. The final section of this chapter on unplanned pathways, lucky breaks and fateful outcomes considers opportunities in relation to access to, fit with and belonging in different graduate labour market spaces. We think about what it means to feel the ease of fitting within graduate employment spaces and what it means to encounter spaces as an outsider or 'space invader' (Puwar, 2004). Following Puwar, we consider what marks some bodies as belonging and others as trespassers. As noted earlier, when Liam made his transition to work, everything felt 'right'. The job felt like it was for him, and the place of employment felt like a good fit. It is a point that he reiterated over the years of his interviews, for example: "When I first did my vacation scheme there, I basically fell in love with the place. When they offered me the job, it was, like, my first offer and, like, the first … I just took it because I knew it was right" (Interview 9). This being and feeling 'right' in a place of work is a significant issue in terms of race, class and gender. Liam is a white, middle-class man who is recognized as belonging through this embodiment of privilege. In Puwar's (2004: 8) terms, he is a body in its right(ful) place: 'Social spaces are not blank and open for anybody to occupy. … Some bodies have the right to belong in certain locations while others are marked out as trespassers who are, in accordance with how both spaces and bodies are imagined, circumscribed as being "out of place".'

Liam has an unmarked body that is 'emptied of gender or race' (Puwar, 2004: 57), which allows him to be a 'fish in water' (Bourdieu and Wacquant, 1992) in elite graduate career spaces. He secured a position where "everything feels right" and where his race, class and gender were accorded recognition through their *invisibility*. For him, "the firm, in particular, felt right", indicating an accord between his habitus and the field. This 'habitus chime' (Ingram, 2018) affords a sense of belonging, or of being in the right place, and confers a feeling of being at ease. The significance of feeling at ease in spaces of value cannot be overestimated, as it is a key component of the process of making and maintaining privilege. Puwar (2004: 57) argues that the power of the privileged body in privileged spaces 'emanates from its ability to be seen as just normal, to be without corporeality'.

The notion of being without corporeality emphasizes that for privileged bodies, attention does not dwell on the body, but instead settles on the mind, allowing a person's qualities/skills to be recognized as cerebral and therefore legitimate. At the same time, privilege becomes misrecognized as competence, which can be considered a process of 'social magic' (Ingram and Allen, 2019). Privilege is transformed into competence through familiarity with the white, male, middle-class body, which paradoxically loses corporeality through skills and competencies being read as emanating from the mind. By contrast, 'other' bodies are hyper-visible, and their corporeality therefore becomes a thing to be considered, rather than denied. Adele provides a striking example of a body that intrudes through hyper-visibility when encountering graduate employment spaces. As we have already discussed earlier, Adele, a mixed-race (African-Caribbean and white), working-class woman, had some struggles in finding her way to a career pathway that met her needs for challenge and stimulation, but she did immediately land a job where she felt connected and had a sense of fit. After three years of working in the charity sector in Bristol, with aspirations for something more challenging, Adele is offered a job as a corporate account manager for a charity based in London. She lands the job after numerous applications and after "about ten" interviews in London, a lot of disappointment and a battle with the "disheartening" nature of the struggle. It is interesting to consider her struggle to find a place of employment in which she could fit in light of the preceding discussion of Liam. Instead of there being a seamless fit between body and space, Adele is marked as a trespasser in the cosmopolitan spaces of the graduate labour market in London, despite having built up significant experience in the sector (something that Liam lacked completely when he gained access to his profession). She recalled some of her experiences of interviews:

> 'As soon as I walked in, I just felt like they had disengaged immediately. I don't know if it's because

they looked at me and thought, "Well, no, we don't like the look."' (Interview 8)

'As soon as I walked in, I think, I was, like, "No, it's not for me", perhaps, I think sometimes, that affects your performance in an interview as well.' (Interview 9)

This tacit recognition of fit works in a dialectical way, what Bourdieu (2002: 31) has referred to as 'a "dialectical confrontation" between habitus as structured structure, and objective structures'. Adele encounters a space in which her body receives cues about its reception, which, in turn, generates the feeling that the place is not right for her. The trespasser feelings impact on performance, as it is difficult to effectively communicate when those who are interpreting your words and your body do not recognize the legitimacy of your 'language'. Through this painful dialectical confrontation, bodies that are marked as 'other' or trespassers learn to align with or reject the structure of the field in which they wish to operate (Ingram and Abrahams, 2016; Ingram, 2018). It took Adele "a long time and a lot of interviews to, kind of, understand what would suit" her, which entailed weathering "a lot of 'No's'" and left her thinking, "Is this for me?" (Interview 10). Despite her experience, her tenacity and a clear plan of direction that emerged over three years, Adele's experiences of rejection in her employment area of choice leave her questioning herself. She wonders if it is for her because she is made to feel that she does not belong.

Adele's efforts finally pay off, and she has a positive interview experience where she met her prospective colleagues before the interview and felt a connection:

'I had to do a presentation; it was one of the best presentations I've done. I was cracking jokes and I had a … you know, we were talking beforehand, like, personally, just about different things, and that kind of set the scene, and it made me a lot more relaxed when I was doing my presentation. But other presentations, like, my leg's been going and I've been really … and I was just like, 'Oh', it just made so much more of a difference.' (Interview 10)

Shilling (1992) stresses the relative values of different forms of physical capital and argues that the dominant class define what is a worthy orientation towards bodily presentation. Concomitantly, he defines corporeal unworthiness, meaning that symbolic violence can be exerted on working-class bodies. Adele's negative interview experiences have transmitted messages of her corporeal unworthiness – her ethnicity, class and gender are worn on her body and have not fitted with that of the employing institution (and, by default, those that comprise the organization). Unlike Liam discussed in this chapter and Luke discussed in Chapter 3, Adele does not get to believe in her own capabilities in a way that is free from doubt. As discussed earlier in the chapter, she constructed her immediate graduate labour market success as luck, while, at the same time, recognizing that she had worked hard for her achievements. In response to her success three years later, she pits the notion of fate against hard work, saying, 'Is it meant to be or was it my hard work?', which is very different to thinking that she is entitled to her success because of her competence and the skills, knowledge and experience she has developed. As we have shown in other chapters in this book, white, middle-class, male graduates are happy to claim their skills and competencies, while also recognizing their privilege; they do not use their privilege to undermine their own success. Adele, on the other hand, partially explains her success through fate. Yet, this fateful outcome for Adele is, in fact, the product of her experiences and decision making, which have been guided by her habitus. In considering the possibility of her outcome being the result of fate, Adele misrecognizes the symbolic violence that she has experienced on the graduate labour market through her embodied racialized, classed and gendered positionality.

At the same time, however, Adele has a sense of the importance of fit and belonging. She strongly emphasizes this at various points when discussing fit with her new place of work and the people she works with. When talking about her manager in work and reflecting on the choices she makes about hiring, Adele tells us: "You have to hire in your mould essentially; you hire people that you think are going to fit into the team. Not only can they do the job, but they can fit into the team" (Interview 10). Adele buys into this hiring in your own image approach, which often does a disservice to those who are not white, middle-class and male (Ingram and

Allen, 2019), because she recognizes the importance of affinity in supporting her career development. In talking of her manager, she says: "She's been career focused and has worked her way up the ladder. She's from a relatively working-class background as well. I feel, like, quite a bit of an affinity with her in that sense as well, as able to, kind of, relate to lots of different people" (Interview 10). She also points to the importance of working with a lot of women who are in positions of power: "We're quite lucky because there's actually quite a lot of females that hire in the organization, like, heads of the teams, there's lots of females, lots of women in high positions at the charity" (Interview 10). While Adele is able to make connections on the basis of class and gender, and to consequently develop clear horizons for action, she does not find 'race affinities' in her employment space. Indeed, she feels her racialized hyper-visibility from the outset of her employment:

'It's so funny, one of my first days there, there was a black guy in the lift with me, and he was, like … he said, "Hello", and I was, like, "Hello", and then he was, like, "Oh, I say, 'Hello' because there's not many of us here; there's not many people of colour here" … and then afterwards, I was, like, "Yeah, he's right, there's hardly any of us here", so, like, we stick out, or you, kind of, notice. But then that's down to the people that were recruiting, and you recruit in your image as well; you recruit in your, kind of. … I think you always recruit people that you have an affinity to.' (Interview 10)

Despite directly discussing the lack of racial diversity in her place of employment, Adele emphasizes definitively that she fits: "I do feel like I fit in. I don't feel like I, kind of, stick out. Even though there's not many of us, I still don't feel that for me, personally, that's an issue, which is good" (Interview 10). Adele simultaneously fits in and stands out across intersectional aspects of embodied identity. She shows incredible flexibility in adapting her embodied performance to the social space she encounters in her employment. The dialectical confrontation of her habitus and the field of her employing institution (which exerts structuring forces that are different to those in which her habitus is structured) generates a productive form of reflexivity that enables Adele to navigate the space as a trespasser who 'passes' and to use her difference to her advantage. She explains this negotiation as follows:

> 'And sometimes, I can have conversations with people, and I'm, like, "You're in a different world to me" or "You grew up in a different world to me." That's not a bad thing; I actually quite like it. I think I can … I play on that quite a bit as well sometimes in my job, which bodes quite well because I think people feel more comfortable. So, I think I flip. So, sometimes, if I'm around people who I know are, like, working class or from that kind of background, I flip back to, like, my language and my behaviour being more, kind of, perhaps … and I feel like, sometimes, my Welsh accent comes out a bit more then as well, so they feel more comfortable with me. But then, if I'm in a meeting, and I'm in a meeting with quite senior people who are quite middle class in their background and how they talk and how they have conversations, then I'll change, and I'll make sure that my tone of voice and my language is more appropriate for that setting. So, I can, kind of, flip between the two, which is quite good.' (Interview 10)

In this example, we see what Ingram (2018) has discussed as a 'reconciled habitus', which is a means of successfully operating in different fields, drawing on different schemes of perception to adjust and adapt ways of being and acting in response to the differing social expectations. Adele's ability to 'flip' requires enormous 'psychic work' (Reay, 2005, 2015) yet affords a means of successfully living with her trespasser status. The ability to have such a 'chameleon habitus' (Abrahams and Ingram, 2013) can be seen as positive, as it allows Adele to find her own way of fitting in. It does, however, come at the cost of intense emotional labour and highlights the inequity of experience for those who are not normalized as being a body in their 'right' place.

Conclusion

> Social experiences are not external influences on
> decision-making they are an integral component of the
> process. (Hodkinson and Sparkes, 1997: 32)

This chapter has highlighted the significance of social experiences,
structured by race, class and gender, in the decisions of graduates
during their first four years after graduation. Despite leaving
university without a specific career plan, each of the four graduates
responded to their unfolding lives in ways that were shaped by the
opportunities arising from their habitus, their social location and
their stocks of capital – what Roberts (1968) refers to as 'opportunity
structures'. These opportunity structures are different for each
individual and flow from levels of privilege or disadvantage, rather
than an objective measure of competence, and they intersect with
perceptions of institutional prestige. They denote the intersections
of the structure of labour markets and structures of advantage/
disadvantage. It is no happy accident that Liam, who is (un)marked
as a white, middle-class, male and a graduate from a Russell Group
university, is able to develop a clear pathway that seems attuned
to his way of being. He is able to use his economically privileged
position to take the time to prepare his path and is able to use his
embodied privilege to ensure his fit. This contrasts with Adele's
experiences of moving into the graduate labour market. Instead of
having time to prepare the ground for her graduate career path, she
has to enter the labour market at the first available entry point and
then orientate herself from there. She has to push back against her
lack of fit and press on when she finds her body to be out of place.

   While all of the graduates discussed in this chapter can be read
as having made it in the hostile world of graduate employment,
the differences in their four-year post-graduation experiences are
striking. The chapter has demonstrated the importance of looking
at the detail of the transition process, rather than simply considering
destination points. The decision making of each of the young adults
in this chapter is directed as much through 'being' as it is through
planning. There are no obvious decision-making crossroads or
'fateful moments' where they have had to choose from a suite of
career options; rather, their choices arise through the everyday

unfolding of their lives, where fateful outcomes and apparent 'lucky breaks' are shaped by the differently available opportunities afforded to those from different class, gender and race backgrounds.

References

Abrahams, J. (2019) Honourable mobility or shameless entitlement? Habitus and graduate employment, *British Journal of Sociology of Education*, 38(5): 625–40.

Abrahams, J. and Ingram, N. (2013) The chameleon habitus: local students' negotiations of multiple fields, *Sociological Research Online*, 18(4): 2, www.socresonline.org.uk/18/4/21.html

Bathmaker, A.M. (2021) Constructing a graduate career future: working with Bourdieu to understand transitions from university to employment for students from working-class backgrounds in England, *European Journal of Education*, 56(1): 78–92.

Bourdieu, P. (2002) Habitus, in J. Hillier and E. Rooksby (eds) *Habitus: A Sense of Place*, Aldershot: Ashgate, pp 27–34.

Bourdieu, P. and Wacquant, L. (1992) *An Invitation to Reflexive Sociology*, Cambridge: Polity.

Giddens, A. (1991) *Modernity and Self-Identity: Self and Society in the Late Modern Age*, Cambridge: Polity.

Glaesser, J. and Cooper, B. (2013) Using rational action theory and Bourdieu's habitus theory together to account for educational decision-making in England and Germany, *Sociology*, 48(3): 463–81.

Goldthorpe, J.H. (2007) *On Sociology, Second Edition, Volume One: Critique and Program*, Stanford, CA: Stanford University Press.

Hodkinson, P. and Sparkes, A. (1997) Careership: a sociological theory of career decision making, *British Journal of Sociology of Education*, 18(1): 29–44.

Holland, J. and Thomson, R. (2009) Gaining perspective on choice and fate, *European Societies*, 11(3): 451–69.

Ingram, N. (2018) *Working-Class Boys and Educational Success: Teenage Identities, Masculinity and Urban Schooling*, Basingstoke: Palgrave Macmillan.

Ingram, N. and Abrahams, J. (2016) Stepping outside of oneself: how a cleft-habitus can lead to greater reflexivity through occupying 'the third space', in J. Thatcher, N. Ingram, C. Burke and J. Abrahams (eds) *Bourdieu: The Next Generation – the Development of Bourdieu's Intellectual Heritage in Contemporary UK Sociology*, BSA Sociological Futures series, Abingdon: Routledge: 140–56.

Ingram, N. and Allen, K. (2019) 'Talent-spotting' or 'social magic'? Inequality, cultural sorting and constructions of the ideal graduate in elite professions, *The Sociological Review*, 67(3): 723–40.

Ingram, N., Abrahams, J. and Bathmaker, A.M. (2018) When class trumps university status: narratives of Zoe and Francesca from the Paired Peers project, in P.J. Burke, A. Hayton and J. Stevenson (eds) *Widening Participation in Higher Education: Towards a Reflexive Approach to Research and Evaluation*, London: Trentham Books, pp 132–52.

Loveday, V. (2017) Luck, chance, and happenstance? Perceptions of success and failure amongst fixed-term academic staff in UK higher education, *British Journal of Sociology*, 11(3): 758–75.

Puwar, N. (2004) *Space Invaders: Race, Gender and Bodies Out of Place*, Oxford: Berg.

Reay, D. (2005) Beyond consciousness? The psychic landscape of social class, *Sociology*, 39(5): 911–28.

Reay, D. (2015) Habitus and the psychosocial: Bourdieu with feelings, *Cambridge Journal of Education*, 45(1): 9–23.

Roberts, K. (1968) The entry into employment: an approach towards a general theory, *The Sociological Review*, 16(2): 165–84.

Shilling, C. (1992) Schooling and the production of physical capital, *Discourse: Studies in the Cultural Politics of Education*, 13(1): 1–19.

9

Conclusion: The Making
of Graduate Lives

Introduction

Throughout this book, we have considered how young graduates construct their transitions to future lives and work, and, at the same time, how they are constructed through those transitions. The making of graduate lives is about profoundly more than finding work. We have shown that there are many ways to be a graduate, and in doing so, we have considered the value that young people place on the work they do and the work to which they aspire. For some, success entailed finding work that required a degree qualification (for example, as a fund-raising officer or project manager in Chapter 8). For others, being a successful graduate entailed finding work that utilized skills and knowledge from their university degree (such as biological knowledge in Chapter 3 and engineering skills in Chapter 5). For yet others, the emphasis was on finding work that they found valuable or meaningful (care work and international development work in Chapter 7; teaching in Chapter 4). The rewards of work in terms of both remuneration and personal satisfaction varied, and there was sometimes a trade-off between the two. The work that graduates constructed as worthy and meaningful was not necessarily well paid, while particularly well-paid work was not often constructed in terms of social value; in one case, the lucrative career of banking was described as 'selling youth'.

While the chapters in the book are based on the narratives of individual participants in the project, this is not merely a set of stories about graduate labour market transitions. Rather, the stories are located within their histories, which consider the connection between structural, institutional and subjective factors in understanding social action and the workings of inequality (Bathmaker, 2010; Burke, 2016; Tarabini and Ingram, 2018). Looking deeply at experiences at the individual level has provided important insight into the reproduction of structural inequalities and how they manifest through the habitus, embodied cultural capital and symbolic classifications that differentiate graduates' value on the labour market.

Labour market futures were not the only consideration for participants in our study; they also talked about how they understood their futures as more than getting a job and achieving a successful career. Relationships with family, significant others and friends were important, and having a social life and enjoying leisure time were part of considerations about what they wanted in their lives. Factors like these played a part in decisions about how to construct a future.

In this concluding chapter, we discuss the ways in which the narrative accounts in the book have allowed us to rethink constructions of graduate success. In what follows: we bring together the ways in which we theorize the significance of the material and the symbolic in graduate employment; we draw attention to how graduate futures are about making a life, not just making a living; and we open up a conversation about re-imagining constructions of graduate success. We finish with reflections on doing longitudinal qualitative inquiry. The Paired Peers team has worked on this project for nearly 12 years. We consider how our lives and work have evolved alongside those of the student and graduate participants in the project during the research process, and we explain how becoming immersed in the lived experience of social class in the 21st century highlights the enduring relevance of understanding and seeking to address social class inequalities.

Material considerations

Building upon the arguments from the first book from this project (Bathmaker et al, 2016), the present book has shown the continued importance of forms of capital (Bourdieu, 1986) in the making of graduate lives. Throughout the chapters in the book, the workings of middle-class privilege have been apparent. This has taken various forms and presents itself in opportunities to live in London, in time to reflect and strategize after graduation, in orientations to travel the world, and in taking risks on hopes and dreams. All of these ways of making a graduate life rely fundamentally on economic capital, and the book has evidenced the importance of material factors in generating the conditions in which transitions can be imagined and decisions can be made. It is important not to underestimate the role of economic capital in structuring horizons for action (Hodkinson and Sparkes, 1997); however, the book has also highlighted the power of symbolic capital in the construction of graduate success.

The symbolic struggle in the construction of the ('right') graduate

To be a graduate is to be constructed as a person of value, a person who has earned a degree and a person who is apparently entitled to labour market and life rewards. However, not all graduates have the same recognition, as the chapters of this book have shown, especially within a highly stratified higher education system like that of the UK. Tholen (2017a, 2017b) argues that being able to construct oneself symbolically as a graduate who is doing graduate work legitimizes social and economic stratification and labour market inequalities:

> The symbolic possession of certified knowledge embodied in university degrees is needed to demarcate groups of workers and enable unequal labour market relations to continue to exist. The current categorization of the labour market shapes how those inside and outside the graduate labour market interpret themselves and the work they perform or do not perform. The hard distinction between graduates and non-graduates, graduate work and non-graduate work is a necessity to keep up the inequality in labour market opportunities and pay differentiation. Validated and recognized by all workers, these associated differences become the basis

of their claims. Symbolic dominance justifies particular groups' or individuals' rewards, occupational protection, or labour conditions. (Tholen, 2017b: 173–4)

In his discussion of symbolic dominance, Tholen develops the concept of *symbolic closure*, itself building on the sociological concept of *social closure* that is used in relation to dominant groups' control of access to resources in a way that justifies their own existence and others' exclusion. Social closure is, in effect, group monopolization of scarce resources, such as money and land. Symbolic closure, on the other hand, considers how power functions through the control of cultural, rather than material, goods. It offers a conceptual framing of the qualities that define graduateness that go beyond the degree certificate. It provides a means for thinking about how some qualities are recognized and afforded value, while others are misrecognized and their value is therefore denied. Here, closure and exclusion operate at the symbolic, rather than material, level through the control of classificatory definitions, rather than tangible resources. Symbolic closure creates the boundaries of a graduate life through demarcating who belongs and who does not belong to the category of 'graduate'. It raises questions about who is considered as displaying 'graduateness', who is a failure in this regard and who is still striving for 'graduate recognition'.

In this book, we have shown a range of ways in which young people come to see themselves as living a meaningful graduate life. In most cases, these conform to the category of graduate success that is constructed through the Graduate Outcomes Survey, which relies on the measure of highly skilled work. In some cases, young people did not measure up to this definition (notably, Jasmine in Chapter 7). The Graduate Outcomes Survey establishes boundaries of recognition and misrecognition, where what (and who) counts as an authentic graduate is consecrated through policy and political discourse. In terms of symbolic closure, this naming of right and wrong, or good and bad graduates, generates a classificatory hierarchy that facilitates the legitimacy (and reward) of some over others. It instils a system of closure and exclusion that functions through the symbolic domain by classifying who belongs to, and who is excluded from, the authentic graduate group. As Bourdieu (2018: 84) highlights:

Raising the question of classification therefore inevitably raises the question of the nature of the group: What is a group? What makes a group? Who has the right to say, 'This is a group'? Which groups have the right to say, 'We are a group'? To whom do groups delegate the right to say, 'This is a group'?

These questions are useful in thinking about the work that is done by policy in signifying what and who determine the nature of the graduate group. Despite an increase in degree-holding labour market participants, the claim to 'graduateness' is not located in knowledge gained, but in labour market conditions, which are a resource that is hoarded and maintained by a select grouping. In this symbolic struggle over graduate legitimacy, certain universities, certain courses and certain graduates from certain backgrounds can all be positioned as worthy or unworthy of graduate status, and therefore entitled or not to the rewards. It is easy to see how this symbolic struggle leads politicians and policy makers into using such language as 'low-value degrees' and to propose policies to shut down courses (and potentially universities) that do not deliver a specific set of labour market outcomes. Symbolic closure through classification of authentic 'graduateness' operates not only to justify the rewards for graduates over their non-graduate peers, but also to generate a hierarchy of graduates that renders a proportion of university leavers as inauthentic. Bourdieu (2018: 83) suggests that those who are able to impose their view of the world by means of determining classification value systems are able to wield power:

> The struggle for symbolic power is therefore a struggle for the imposition of a principle of perception of the world, a principle of classification and division, diacritics, criticism and judgment, that should be acknowledged to be legitimate. This principle is grounded in the *consensus ominium*, and in return derives from this consensus a form of objectivity.

The consensus of graduate value allows for differential labour market rewards for those who display certain characteristics that have been preordained as worthy of reward. These may take the form of confidence, deportment or the 'right' qualifications from the 'right' universities, and may not necessarily relate to any specific skill set or knowledge. In this way, characteristics not only usurp skills and knowledge, but also become read as objective evidence of their existence. This transformation or usurpation has been referred to as an act of 'social magic', transubstantiation or consecration, where one thing becomes read as something else and, in doing so, comes to be seen as objective and legitimate. Elite graduate employers seek nebulous characteristics like 'Googliness' or 'personal brand' from candidates as a means of displaying distinction from the graduate mass, and these performances of fit allow organizations to select their recruits according to cultural homologies, rather than evidence of technical competence (Ho, 2009; Rivera, 2015; Ingram and Allen, 2019). Through a process of social magic, cultural display becomes a signifier of competence, which is, in the final instance, transformed into a seemingly objective perception of competence itself.

This can be seen across the chapters of this book where graduates are ordained or rejected on the basis of their embodied performances and/or assumed brilliance or lack of it. In Chapter 3, for example, Luke is open about how his degree qualification from an 'elite' Russell Group university and embodied white, male, middle-class privilege are read as his potential competence for a job for which he neither holds technical qualifications nor possesses relevant experience. This contrasts with the experience of Adele in Chapter 8, whose embodied capital is misrecognized as lack of fit and competence, resulting in multiple rejections in interviews for graduate jobs.

Symbolic closure and social magic within the field of graduate struggles: the embodiment of privilege

Within the field of graduate struggles, embodied symbolic capital asserts itself as a distinguishing force when other forms of capital are comparable. It is in this realm of the symbolic that classification and the power to classify engender the maintenance of inequality. Those who are the arbiters of capital determine the value of cultural performances, ultimately leading to the privileging of the embodied performances that align with those who determine their value. In other words, employers employ in their own image and value those who conform to their own cultural practices. At the same time, they misrecognize embodied performances that are outside their cultural register and are not only unlikely to see their value, but also likely to subscribe a *lack* of value to the alien bodies they perceive. These space invaders (Puwar, 2004) generate a discomfort of cultural misalignment that can only be reasonably explained by their inherent wrongness. To think otherwise would require those who are privileged to confront the arbitrariness of their value. In this way, power relations become somatized and lived out in everyday bodily interactions. As McNay (2007: 91) argues: 'Embodiment is not a one-sided process where the somatization of power relations ensures the blind conformity of individuals to social structures. It is also an active process of self-realization, of "living through" the tendencies of the world that have been incorporated into the body.' Symbolic dominance becomes legitimated and actualized through bodies that have, on the one hand, incorporated and, on the other, themselves produced structures of dominance. Bodies, therefore, achieve degrees of recognition and misrecognition within the field of (in this case, graduate labour market) struggles. Through recognition, misrecognition and classificatory struggles, bodies are also rendered as belonging or being out of place in the graduate labour market. This spatializing of belonging, outlined most powerfully by Puwar (2004) in her book *Space Invaders*, which involves intersections of race, class and gender, constructs some bodies as a 'natural' fit and others as out of place, as explored in Chapters 3, 5 and 8.

Making a life, not just making a living

The life that 'the degree generation' chooses to live is not just about graduate employment. Throughout the pages of this book, we have shown how important it was for the young people in our study to find meaningful work and to live a life of personal value. This took different forms for different people: for some, it meant building a life in the locality where they grew up in order to be close to family (see Chapter 4); for others, it meant adventure and travel (see Chapters 4 and 7). For some, finding highly paid work was what they valued (see Chapter 6); for others, it was finding work of social worth (see Chapter 7). Many, though, placed value in finding work they enjoyed, though this was not realizable for all. As time passed, for some, the initial optimism at the point of graduation wore off and they were starting to feel disillusioned by work, especially in cases where their dreams and aspirations were not supported by the reality of the labour market. Most notably, Jasmine (see Chapter 7) struggled to realize the graduate life she had optimistically envisioned for herself. Tholen (2017a: 1078) critiques the social fiction that a degree leads to a fulfilling career:

> Within the graduate labour pool, members accept the social fiction that disguises the failure of many graduates to lead fulfilling careers, high wages and skilled jobs. Graduates and groups of graduates need to continuously convince others of their value and (re)negotiate the meaning and value of (particular) qualifications, skills, occupations and careers.

There are many ways to be a graduate and to live a graduate life, a point that is lost in policy discussions that focus narrowly on employment outcomes, measured by work that is deemed to be highly skilled. Policy neglects to consider the actual work that many graduates do, which is often work that non-graduates also do, work that involves low pay and a struggle to make ends meet and to make a life. The link between making a living and making a life for younger generations needs to be better understood in the policy domain, especially in relation to inequalities.

Re-imagining constructions of graduate success

Throughout this book, we have shown the importance of symbolic capital in a four-year period of transition to and through the graduate labour market for working-class and middle-class students who attended one of two universities in the same city, institutions differently positioned within a highly stratified system of higher education. Each chapter has focused on a different theme that emerged from the data analysis, and together, the chapters provide a picture of the complex ways in which graduates navigate their early careers and how inequalities manifest in the transition process. We have used a Bourdieusian approach to explore the ways in which different forms of capital are mobilized to secure advantage, as well as how embodied forms of capital can work for and against young people in the graduate labour market field. In this chapter, we have drawn together the theoretical threads used in our analysis and offer an original contribution to thinking about contemporary graduate labour market transitions. Building upon the work of Tholen (2017a and b), Ingram and Allen (2019) and Puwar (2004), and using Bourdieu's overall theoretical framework – in particular, his recently translated lectures from the 1980s on classification struggles (Bourdieu, 2018) – we bring together the concepts of symbolic closure, social magic and embodiment in a unique way. This has allowed us to show how symbolic classifications generate symbolic closure through processes of both social magic and embodiment. The resulting hierarchy of value renders certain graduates as bearers of high value and positions others as holding low value.

Capital is symbolically legitimated by those who are set to gain the most from its consecration as a capital of value. In other words, the privileged use the symbolic domain to construct value and maintain their own privilege. As Bourdieu (2018: 87) observes:

> One level of social existence, then, is a _percepi_, a being perceived, and symbolic capital is a form of perceived being which implies that those who do the perceiving acknowledge recognition of those whom they perceive. We might say that one of the goals of the symbolic struggle is to change the mode of actual being by changing the way that being is perceived, since perceived being is part of the truth of our being in the social world.

These perceptions and recognitions generate a social order that allows advantage to be maintained and inequalities to persist. In terms of graduate labour market transitions, they can operate through capabilities for geographical mobility (see Chapters 3 and 4), orientations towards geographical mobility (see Chapter 4), confidence, aspiration and the performance of competence (see Chapters 5 and 7), the capacity for risk taking and entrepreneurialism (see Chapter 6), and cultural fit (see Chapter 8). Perceived being generates a reality that legitimates labour market inequalities as the objective end point of a meritocratic process. Bourdieu (2018: 87) orientates us to 'change the mode of actual being by changing the way that being is perceived', suggesting that change in the symbolic domain is necessary for a shift in patterns of inequality.

The construction of a graduate of value, therefore, relies on a recognition of the middle-class habitus and a valuing of a 'good' middle-class life. The 'mode of actual being' referred to by Bourdieu is a middle-class mode, where what is valued involves middle-class ways of being. The corollary of this is the misrecognition of those who are 'other'. We have seen this in operation in the chapters of this book where white middle-class advantage is strongly at work in the making of graduate lives and working-class and racialized others struggle for recognition.

Doing longitudinal qualitative inquiry

This book is the culmination of a research project that has spanned nearly 12 years. The research team of 11 people came together out of a shared concern to explore and understand better the workings of social class for 'the degree generation'. Specifically, we wanted to follow the lives of young people from working-class backgrounds who appeared to achieve mobility through participation in higher education and compare their experience with peers from middle-class backgrounds, for whom higher education was a means of consolidating class position. Doing longitudinal qualitative inquiry was a way of illuminating what troubles us: the processes through which inequalities not only endure, but may also be challenged and overcome (Bathmaker, 2010). We were interested in the relation between individual agency and social structure, and how these relations were experienced by the degree generation.

As a research team, we are from a variety of social class backgrounds, and our own experience of higher education and progression on to future lives resonates with the participants in the project from working-class backgrounds in some cases and with those from middle-class backgrounds in others. Eight of us are women, while three are men. We are all white. We are from a range of different generations: from post-Second World War babies and baby boomers to children of the 1970s and 1980s. While we worked and lived in Bristol at the time of the project, our home places include England, Wales, the north of Ireland and Greece. Five of the team members were involved in the project from the beginning right through to the end, three were involved in the second phase of the project and three were part of the project for a short period of time. Together, we bring with us a history of experiences that offer different perspectives on class, race and gender, which have been grappled with to arrive at the final analysis offered in this and in our previous book (Bathmaker et al, 2016).

The project took place during tumultuous times. It started in 2010, just as New Labour's 13 years in power came to an end, to be replaced by a coalition Conservative–Liberal Democrat government in the UK. The following years were marked by: the austerity politics of the Coalition government and the introduction of £9,000 higher education tuition fees to be paid by students from 2012; Brexit, with the UK finally leaving the EU in January 2020 under what was, by then, a Conservative government led by Boris Johnson; a global climate crisis; the worldwide COVID-19 pandemic from 2020; the evacuation of Afghanistan in 2021; and the war in Ukraine which started in 2022. All these events have played out in different ways in the lives of the Paired Peers graduates, as well as the Paired Peers research team.

In conducting the research, we became very absorbed in the lived experiences of our participants as they shared the intimacies of their thoughts and experiences over a significant period of time in their young adult lives. During the course of these years, while we maintained positions of robust and rigorous researchers, we could not help but feel invested in the plans, hopes and dreams of our participants as their lives unfolded. In writing this final analysis, it has been both joyous and painful to explore the struggles and successes of the participants in the Paired Peers project. Our aim has been to make sense of the lives as lived by our participants and, in writing about their experience, to highlight and critique taken-for-granted practices and structural and cultural features of the everyday social worlds of undergraduate study and progression to graduate lives. In doing so, we have sought to make visible the workings of power and the spaces and limitations for the taking of power through individual agency. In following the workings of class for the degree generation, we have shown the persistence of intersecting class-, race- and gender-based inequalities. At the same time, the experiences of the Paired Peers graduates open up possibilities for re-imagining the meaning of graduate success in the 21st century. Graduate outcomes are becoming increasingly important in terms of how universities are held to account by the UK's OfS, and at the time of writing (late 2022), there is considerable policy talk about the value of degrees. A discourse of value for money prevails that is often attached to employment outcomes and earnings. What is missing from policy-level discussions of graduate success, particularly in the UK, is a recognition of what it means to live a graduate life, what graduates gain from an experience of education that challenges them to think about the sort of citizens they want to be in society, the values they take with them and their hopes for their futures and the future of the world they want to live in.

References

Bathmaker, A.M. (2010) Introduction, in A.M. Bathmaker and P. Harnett (eds) *Exploring Learning, Identity and Power through Life History and Narrative Research*, London: Routledge, pp 1–10.

Bathmaker, A.M., Ingram, N., Abrahams, J., Hoare, A., Waller, R. and Bradley, H. (2016) *Higher Education, Social Class and Social Mobility: The Degree Generation*, London: Palgrave Macmillan.

Bourdieu, P. (1986) The forms of capital, in J. Richardson (ed), *Handbook of Theory and Research for the Sociology of Education*, Westport, CT: Greenwood, pp 241–58.

Bourdieu, P. (2018) *Classification Struggles*, Cambridge: Polity.

Burke, C. (2016) *Culture, Capitals and Graduate Futures: Degrees of Class*, London: Routledge and Society for Research into Higher Education.

Ho, K.Z. (2009) *Liquidated: An Ethnography of Wall Street*, Durham, NC: Duke University Press.

Hodkinson, P. and Sparkes, A. (1997) Careership: a sociological theory of career decision making, *British Journal of Sociology of Education*, 18(1): 29–44.

Ingram, N. and Allen, K. (2019) 'Talent-spotting' or 'social magic'? Inequality, cultural sorting and constructions of the ideal graduate in elite professions, *The Sociological Review*, 67(3): 723–40.

McNay, L. (2007) *Against Recognition*, Cambridge: Polity.

Puwar, N. (2004) *Space Invaders: Race, Gender and Bodies Out of Place*, Oxford: Berg.

Rivera, L. (2015) *Pedigree: How Elite Students Get Elite Jobs*, Princeton, NJ: Princeton University Press.

Tarabini, A. and Ingram, N. (2018) *Educational Choices, Transitions and Aspirations in Europe: Systemic, Institutional and Subjective Challenges*, Abingdon: Routledge.

Tholen, G. (2017a) Symbolic closure: towards a renewed sociological perspective on the relationship between higher education, credentials and the graduate labour market, *Sociology*, 51(5): 1067–83.

Tholen, G. (2017b) *Graduate Work*, Oxford: Oxford University Press.

Appendix

Table A.1: The employment destinations of the Paired Peers participants at the final interview

Name	Gender	Social class	University	Undergraduate subject	Job at the time of Interview 10
Carly	F	M	UoB	Economics/accounting/finance	Client support at a finance company
Cerys	F	M	UoB	History	Regional education contact officer
Freya	F	M	UoB	Biology	Working for an institute that specializes in wildlife conservation
Hannah	F	M	UoB	Psychology	Studying for Bachelor of Medicine (MBChB)
Jenifer	F	M	UoB	Engineering	Engineer
Lauren	F	M	UoB	Sociology	1. Waitress at a delicatessen/cafe (part-time) 2. Freelance work for a charity consultant
Rose	F	M	UoB	Drama	Office administrator for a small-/medium-sized enterprise (SME)
Sally	F	M	UoB	Law	Secondary school teacher
Scarlett	F	M	UoB	Geography	Primary school teacher
Amelia	F	W	UoB	Biology	1. English teaching assistant 2. Private tutoring

Table A.1: The employment destinations of the Paired Peers participants at the final interview (continued)

Name	Gender	Social class	University	Undergraduate subject	Job at the time of Interview 10
Anna	F	W	UoB	Politics	Risk analyst
Bianca	F	W	UoB	History	Secondary school teacher
Connie	F	W	UoB	Drama/English	Document formatter and editorial trainee for a small educational resources publisher
Jackie	F	W	UoB	Sociology	Primary school teacher
Jade	F	W	UoB	Psychology	Investment consultant
Lizzie	F	W	UoB	Engineering	Engineer
Megan	F	W	UoB	English	Secondary school teacher
Melissa	F	W	UoB	English	Blogger for a well-known Internet forum
Samantha	F	W	UoB	Geography	PhD study
Zoe	F	W	UoB	Law	Paralegal
Adrian	M	M	UoB	Economics/accounting/finance	Industrial PhD fellow (50 per cent funded by bank)
Craig	M	M	UoB	Engineering	Design engineer

(continued)

Table A.1: The employment destinations of the Paired Peers participants at the final interview (continued)

Name	Gender	Social class	University	Undergraduate subject	Job at the time of Interview 10
Elliot	M	M	UoB	English	Journalist on a national newspaper
Harry	M	M	UoB	Politics	1. Administrative assistant 3. Delivery service (Deliveroo) 4. MA in International Politics
Liam	M	M	UoB	Politics	Lawyer
Luke	M	M	UoB	Biology	Computer programmer at an investment company
Martin	M	M	UoB	Sociology	Officer at a development charity
Nathan	M	M	UoB	Law	Investment executive (own company)
Sebastian	M	M	UoB	Geography	Senior consultant/assistant manager at an international audit company
Garry	M	W	UoB	History	Project manager at an international professional services company
Harvey	M	W	UoB	Economics/accounting/finance	Recruitment consultant/headhunter
Justin	M	W	UoB	Psychology	Primary school teacher

Table A.1: The employment destinations of the Paired Peers participants at the final interview (continued)

Name	Gender	Social class	University	Undergraduate subject	Job at the time of Interview 10
Marcus	M	W	UoB	Engineering	Engineer
Sean	M	W	UoB	Politics	English teacher (overseas)
Tony	M	W	UoB	Economics/accounting/ finance	Finance analyst
Amber	F	M	UWE	Engineering	Secondary school teacher
Francesca	F	M	UWE	Law	Manager at an insurance company
Harriet	F	M	UWE	English	1. Internship for a London lifestyle magazine 2. Temping administrative work
Joanna	F	M	UWE	Psychology	Police officer
Lilly	F	M	UWE	History	Mentor working for a church
Lynn	F	M	UWE	Drama	Further education teacher
Adele	F	W	UWE	History	Charity corporate fundraiser
Jasmine	F	W	UWE	Sociology	Unemployed
Ruby	F	W	UWE	English	Primary school teacher

(continued)

Table A.1: The employment destinations of the Paired Peers participants at the final interview (continued)

Name	Gender	Social class	University	Undergraduate subject	Job at the time of Interview 10
Sophie	F	W	UWE	Politics	Administrator at a large national company
Christopher	M	M	UWE	Law	Trainee solicitor
Dylan	M	M	UWE	Politics	Currency trader
Jeff	M	M	UWE	Sociology	Teaching assistant at a primary school
Lloyd	M	M	UWE	Drama	Assistant public relations officer for a city council
Nicholas	M	M	UWE	Engineering	Engineer
Oscar	M	M	UWE	Politics	Paramedic ambulance service
Charlie	M	W	UWE	History	Financial consultant for a national company
Kyle	M	W	UWE	Law	Paralegal
Leo	M	W	UWE	Economics/accounting/finance	Research finance administrator in a university
Rob	M	W	UWE	Engineering	Engineer
Shane	M	W	UWE	Economics/accounting/finance	Economist

Note: Gender: M = male; F = female. Social class: M = middle class; W = working class

Index

engineering 95
engineering capital 93, 97, 100,
    101, 103
London 56, 58, 59, 60, 62
nebulous characteristics sought 179
spatialization of belonging 180
unplanned fateful outcomes 165–7,
    168–9
flexibility 81, 82, 91, 145–6
Freya 47, 52–8
Friedman, S. 45, 67, 82, 95
Futuretrack 20, 132

G

Gale, T. 71, 72, 73, 74, 81
Gamsu, S. 12, 13, 82, 129, 140
gap years 54, 141
Garry 160, 162–5
gender
    corporeal unworthiness 168
    engineering 88–107
    'right' fit 165
    'top boys' in the finance
        sector 108–28
gender diversity 33–4
Generation X 8
geographical mobility 65–87, 182
Giddens, A. 14, 155
Gillborn, D. 36
'giving something back' 133
global acumen 46, 53, 98–9
global cultural capital 146
global labour markets 146
globalization 108, 145
Goldthorpe, J.H. 13, 15, 130,
    131, 161
"good life" 14
graduate employment schemes
    44–64, 99–100, 123, 157, 163
'graduate jobs' 3
'graduate labour markets' 3,
    13, 181–2
Graduate Outcomes surveys 2, 3, 10,
    30, 39, 177
Gram, M. 81

H

habitus
    Bourdieusian 15
    chameleon habitus 70, 170
    defined 14
    dialectical confrontation 167,
        169–70

effect on fateful outcomes 168
elite metropolitan privilege 55–6
gendered 91
habitus chime 165
habitus-to-field adjustment 35
home 66
home as 70–1
'London habitus' 46, 53, 54, 58, 61
middle classes as mode of actual
    being 183
predisposition versus
    predetermination 70
reconciled habitus 170
spatial mobility 69–73
staying in home area 68
in the transition process 156
see also 'fit'
hard work 14, 45, 73, 75, 77, 94,
    161, 168
Harris, A. 109, 110
Harvey 109, 111, 116–22
headhunting 59, 61, 114, 120
Hebson, G. 32
hegemonic masculinities 126
Henderson, H. 69
Higher Education Careers Service
    Unit 67
Higher Education Statistical Agency
    (HESA) 4, 30
Hodkinson, P. 15, 159, 161, 171, 176
Holdsworth, C. 70
Holland, J. 7, 14–15
Hollingworth, S. 68, 70, 81
Holmes, J. 91
home
    as base 81
    differing concepts of 80–1
    graduate mobilities and spatial
        belonging 65–87
    living in family home as means to
        take low-paid work 54
    as 'local capital' 69
    pre-university London 48–9,
        50, 52–3
    returning to family home 53, 55,
        65, 67–9, 117, 136, 142, 155–6
hot knowledge 126
humour 91, 96
hyper-visible bodies 166, 169

I

imagined futures 76–7
increasing participation 12, 130–1

.